Nutribullet Recipe Book

Nature's Bounty: Nutribullet Recipes for Nutrient-Rich Smoothies

By

Latasha W. Villagomez

Table of Contents

- INTRODUCTION TO NUTRIBULLET NUTRITION 9
- ENERGIZING BREAKFAST BLENDS: 13
  - SUNRISE CITRUS BURST: 13
  - BANANA BERRY BLAST: 13
  - OATMEAL COOKIE SMOOTHIE: 14
  - TROPICAL TURMERIC DELIGHT: 14
  - GREEN ENERGY BOOSTER: 15
  - ALMOND DATE BREAKFAST SHAKE: 16
  - PEANUT BUTTER BANANA POWER SMOOTHIE: 16
  - MANGO COCONUT MORNING BLISS: 17
  - BLUEBERRY SPINACH SUPERCHARGE: 18
  - COFFEE LOVER'S WAKE-UP CALL: 19
- REFRESHING SMOOTHIE BOWLS: 19
  - ACAI BERRY BOWL WITH GRANOLA CRUNCH: 19
  - GREEN GODDESS BOWL WITH KIWI AND CHIA SEEDS: 20
  - DRAGON FRUIT DELIGHT BOWL: 21
  - RASPBERRY COCONUT BLISS BOWL: 22
  - TROPICAL MANGO-PINEAPPLE PARADISE BOWL: 23
  - BERRY BLAST SMOOTHIE BOWL WITH ALMONDS: 23
  - KIWI-BANANA SMOOTHIE BOWL WITH FLAX SEEDS: 24
  - PITAYA (DRAGON FRUIT) AND BANANA BOWL: 25
  - PEANUT BUTTER CHOCOLATE SMOOTHIE BOWL: 26
  - GREEN TEA AND BERRY BLAST BOWL: 27
- NUTRIENT-PACKED GREEN SMOOTHIES: 28
  - KALE-PINEAPPLE GREEN REVIVER: 28
  - CUCUMBER MINT GREEN REFRESHER: 28
  - SPINACH AVOCADO DREAM: 29
  - DETOXIFYING GREEN ELIXIR: 30
  - ZESTY GREEN GINGERADE: 30

- GREEN GRAPES AND HONEYDEW MELON BLEND: 31
- KIWI-KALE SUPER GREENS SMOOTHIE: 31
- GREEN GODDESS PROTEIN SHAKE: 32
- BROCCOLI-APPLE GREEN DELIGHT: 33
- MINTY GREEN WATERMELON COOLER: 33

IMMUNITY BOOSTING BLENDS: 34

- CITRUS IMMUNE DEFENDER: 34
- GINGER-TURMERIC ANTIOXIDANT BLAST: 34
- BERRY ANTIVIRAL BOOSTER: 35
- PINEAPPLE-ORANGE COLD BUSTER: 36
- ELDERBERRY AND BLUEBERRY IMMUNE ELIXIR: 36
- CARROT-GINGER IMMUNITY BLEND: 37
- GREEN APPLE-ECHINACEA BOOST: 37

PROTEIN-PACKED POWER BLENDS: 39

- ALMOND BUTTER BANANA PROTEIN SHAKE: 39
- CHOCOLATE PEANUT BUTTER POWERHOUSE: 40
- CHIA SEED AND RASPBERRY PROTEIN BOOST: 41
- GREEK YOGURT BERRY BLAST: 41
- HEMP SEED PROTEIN PARADISE: 42
- VANILLA COCONUT PROTEIN SMOOTHIE: 43
- SPIRULINA PROTEIN POWER PUNCH: 43
- QUINOA-BERRY PROTEIN SHAKE: 44
- PUMPKIN SEED PROTEIN ELIXIR: 45
- SPINACH-TOFU PROTEIN SUPERCHARGE: 45

SUPERFOOD ELIXIRS AND SHOTS: 46

- TURMERIC-GINGER WELLNESS SHOT: 46
- WHEATGRASS AND LEMON DETOX ELIXIR: 47
- SPIRULINA ENERGIZING SHOT: 47
- MATCHA GREEN TEA ANTIOXIDANT ELIXIR: 48
- CHIA SEED HYDRATION SHOT: 49
- ALOE VERA DIGESTIVE SOOTHER: 49
- CACAO MACA MOOD BOOSTER: 50
- GOJI BERRY BEAUTY ELIXIR: 51
- CAMU CAMU VITAMIN C SHOT: 51
- MORINGA MINT DETOX SHOT: 52

NUTRIBULLET NUT BUTTER CREATIONS: 52
- Classic Homemade Almond Butter: 52
- Cinnamon-Vanilla Cashew Butter: 53
- Maple-Pecan Butter Bliss: 54
- Chocolate-Hazelnut Indulgence: 55
- Creamy Coconut Macadamia Butter: 56
- Honey-Roasted Peanut Butter: 56
- Spicy Cacao Brazil Nut Butter: 57
- Vanilla-Walnut Butter Delight: 58
- Salted Pistachio Butter Infusion: 59
- Espresso-Sesame Seed Butter: 60

HEALTHY SNACKS AND DIPS: 61
- Creamy Avocado Hummus: 61
- Greek Yogurt Spinach Dip: 61
- Roasted Red Pepper and Walnut Dip: 62
- Zucchini Fries with Lemon-Dill Dip: 63
- Spicy Chickpea Snack Mix: 64
- Cucumber Slices with Tzatziki Sauce: 65
- Sweet Potato Chips with Guacamole: 66
- Buffalo Cauliflower Bites: 67
- Carrot and Beetroot Dip: 68
- Edamame and Mint Hummus: 69

DETOX AND CLEANSING BLENDS: 70
- Green Detoxifying Elixir: 70
- Lemon Ginger Cleanser: 70
- Detoxifying Beet Blast: 71
- Cleansing Cucumber-Mint Cooler: 71
- Blueberry-Cabbage Detox Blend: 72
- Pineapple-Matcha Detox Smoothie: 73
- Ginger-Lemon Apple Cleanse: 73
- Cranberry Detox Refresher: 74
- Turmeric Detox Powerhouse: 74
- Papaya-Parsley Cleansing Blend: 75

INDULGENT DESSERT SMOOTHIES: 76

- CHOCOLATE BANANA DREAM SHAKE: 76
- VANILLA ALMOND DATE SMOOTHIE: 76
- STRAWBERRY CHEESECAKE DELIGHT: 77
- MINT CHOCOLATE CHIP INDULGENCE: 78
- PEANUT BUTTER CUP OF SMOOTHIE: 78
- RASPBERRY WHITE CHOCOLATE BLISS 79
- BLACK FOREST CHERRY SMOOTHIE 80
- COCONUT MANGO SORBET SHAKE 80
- COOKIES AND CREAM FANTASY 81
- SALTED CARAMEL PRETZEL DELIGHT 81

HYDRATING SUMMER SIPS: 82
- WATERMELON-LIME COOLER: 82
- PINEAPPLE MINT REFRESHER: 83
- CUCUMBER-LEMONADE SPLASH: 84
- HONEYDEW-BASIL BREEZE: 84
- MANGO-PEACH ICED TEA: 85
- RASPBERRY-LEMON SPARKLER: 86
- BLUEBERRY-LAVENDER LEMONADE: 86
- KIWI-COCONUT WATER QUENCHER: 87
- STRAWBERRY-BASIL INFUSED WATER: 88
- CITRUSY HIBISCUS PUNCH: 88

NUTRIBULLET MOCKTAILS: NON-ALCOHOLIC BLENDS: 89
- VIRGIN PIÑA COLADA: 89
- STRAWBERRY MOJITO MOCKTAIL: 90
- BLUEBERRY BASIL SMASH: 91
- CUCUMBER COOLER MOCKTAIL: 91
- PEACH BELLINI MOCKTAIL: 92
- SPARKLING CRANBERRY LIMEADE: 93
- RASPBERRY MINT FIZZ: 93
- COCONUT LIME MOCKTAIL: 94
- KIWI SPARKLER: 95
- MANGO-GINGER MOCKTAIL: 96

BOOSTING BRAIN HEALTH WITH NUTRIBULLET: 96
- BRAIN-BOOSTING BERRY BLAST: 96
- WALNUT-BLUEBERRY BRAIN FUEL: 97

- Spinach and Flax Memory Enhancer: 98
- Turmeric-Ginger Cognitive Kick: 98
- Almond and Dark Chocolate Cognition Elixir: 99
- Kale and Walnut Neuro-Nourisher: 100
- f. Avocado Brainpower Smoothie: 100
- Coconut-Berry Brain Booster: 101
- Chia Seed Omega-3 Smoothie: 102
- Pumpkin Seed Brain Blend: 102

NUTRIBULLET FOR WEIGHT MANAGEMENT: 103

- Green Protein Power Shake: 103
- Berry-Banana Weight Loss Smoothie: 104
- Almond Butter and Spinach Smoothie: 105
- Chia Seed and Berry Slimdown Shake: 105
- Avocado and Kale Weight Buster: 106

SPECIAL DIETARY CONSIDERATIONS: GLUTEN-FREE, VEGAN, ETC.: 107

- Quinoa and Roasted Vegetable Salad (Gluten-Free, Vegan): 107
- Cauliflower Rice Stir-Fry (Gluten-Free, Vegan): 108
- Chickpea and Vegetable Curry (Gluten-Free, Vegan): 109
- Zucchini Noodles with Avocado Pesto (Gluten-Free, Vegan): 110
- Lentil and Spinach Soup (Gluten-Free, Vegan): 111
- Portobello Mushroom Burger (Gluten-Free, Vegan): 112
- Vegan Pad Thai with Tofu (Gluten-Free, Vegan): 113
- Spinach and Artichoke Quinoa Bites (Gluten-Free, Vegan): 115
- Mexican Stuffed Bell Peppers (Gluten-Free, Vegan): 116

NUTRIBULLET RECIPES FOR KIDS: 118

- Banana-Berry Blast Smoothie: 118
- Hidden Veggie Tomato Sauce: 119
- Cheesy Cauliflower Tots: 119
- Apple Cinnamon Oatmeal Bites: 120
- Green Monster Popsicles (with spinach and fruit): 121
- Mini Veggie Frittatas: 122
- Peanut Butter and Jelly Smoothie: 123
- Sweet Potato Fries with Dipping Sauce: 124
- Veggie Rainbow Wraps with Hummus: 125
- Strawberry-Banana FrOuncesen Yogurt Bites: 125

ANTI-INFLAMMATORY BLENDS: 126

    TURMERIC AND GINGER IMMUNITY SHOT: 126
    PINEAPPLE-TURMERIC SMOOTHIE: 127
    MANGO-TURMERIC LASSI: 127
    GOLDEN MILK ELIXIR: 128
    GREEN TEA AND BERRY ANTIOXIDANT BLEND: 129
    BLUEBERRY-GINGER ANTI-INFLAMMATORY SMOOTHIE: 129
    KALE AND PINEAPPLE ANTI-INFLAMMATORY JUICE: 130
    PAPAYA AND TURMERIC DIGESTIVE SOOTHER: 131
    CUCUMBER AND ALOE VERA COOLER: 131
    SPINACH AND CHERRY INFLAMMATION BUSTER: 132

BEAUTY FROM WITHIN: SMOOTHIES FOR RADIANT SKIN AND HAIR 133

    BERRY BEAUTY BOOSTER: 133
    GREEN GODDESS GLOW: 134
    MANGO MELON MAGIC: 134
    CITRUS RADIANCE REFRESHER: 135
    POMEGRANATE PARADISE: 136
    SILKY SILICA SMOOTHIE: 137
    BERRY GLOW RADIANCE 137
    AVOCADO COLLAGEN BOOSTER 138
    CARROT ORANGE RADIANCE 138
    SPINACH BLUEBERRY BEAUTY 139
    COCONUT CUCUMBER HYDRATOR 140

ENERGIZING NUTRIBLASTS: BEAT THE AFTERNOON SLUMP 140

    COFFEE KICKSTART: 140
    POWER-PACKED GREEN ENERGY: 141
    CHOCO-BANANA BOOST: 141
    NUTTY PROTEIN PUNCH: 142
    TROPICAL TURMERIC REFUEL: 143
    ENERGIZING ESPRESSO SHAKE: 143
    ESPRESSO PROTEIN BOOST: 144
    MATCHA ENERGY ELIXIR: 145
    CITRUS WAKE-UP CALL: 146
    CHIA SEED POWER-UP: 146
    MANGO TANGO ZING: 147

DESSERT-INSPIRED SMOOTHIES: GUILT-FREE INDULGENCE 148

- Chocolate-Almond Dream: 148
- Berry Cheesecake Delight:..149
- Caramel Apple Crisp:..149
- Mint Chocolate Chip Bliss: 150
- Peach Cobbler Concoction: 151
- Lemon-Blueberry Pie:...152

CLEANSING DETOX BLASTS: RENEW AND RESET 157

- Green Detox Elixir: 157
- Beetroot Cleanse: 157
- Lemon-Ginger Flush: 158
- Detoxifying Dandelion Greens: 159
- Berry Detox Blast:..159
- Turmeric Cleanse: 160

NUTRIBULLET COCKTAILS: HEALTHY LIBATIONS FOR SOCIAL GATHERINGS 164

- Tropical Tequila Tango: 164
- Mojito Twist: 164
- Berry Vodka Crush: 165
- Spicy Paloma Punch: 166
- Cucumber Gin Refresher:..167
- Pomegranate Whiskey Sour:...167
- Tropical Turmeric Twist: 168
- Berry Mojito Madness:..168
- Cucumber Ginger Refresher:...169
- Spicy Watermelon Punch: 170
- Pomegranate Basil Fizz:...170

INTRODUCTION TO NUTRIBULLET NUTRITION

1.1 What is the Nutribullet? The Nutribullet is a revolutionary kitchen appliance designed to extract the maximum nutritional value from fruits, vegetables, nuts, and seeds. Unlike traditional blenders that may leave behind pulp and fiber or juicers that remove essential nutrients, Nutribullet's unique extraction technology breaks down ingredients into a smooth and easily digestible form. The powerful motor and high-speed blending action ensure that every part of the ingredients is utilized, resulting in nutrient-rich and delicious smoothies called "Nutriblasts."

1.2 Benefits of Using a Nutribullet Incorporating the Nutribullet into your daily routine offers many health benefits. One of the key advantages is better nutrient absorption. The Nutribullet allows the body to absorb more nutrients efficiently by breaking down food into its most digestible form. Additionally, Nutriblasts are packed with fiber, promoting digestive health and regularity.

The Nutribullet also provides a convenient way to increase fruit and vegetable intake, even for those who struggle to consume enough daily servings. By blending various fruits and vegetables into delicious and visually appealing smoothies, the Nutribullet makes healthy eating more enjoyable.

Moreover, Nutribullet promotes weight management by supporting a feeling of fullness and reducing unhealthy snacking habits. The recipes in this book are designed to be satisfying and nutrient-dense, making them an excellent

Lastly, the Nutribullet is a versatile appliance that can be used to make Nutriblasts and soups, sauces, nut butter, and more. This makes it a valuable tool in any kitchen, regardless of dietary preferences.

1.3 How the Nutribullet Works Understanding how the Nutribullet works is essential for getting the most out of this appliance. Its robust motor and unique blade design are the core of the Nutribullet's effectiveness. When ingredients are loaded into the cup of, and the base is activated, the high-speed blending action breaks down the cell walls of fruits, vegetables, nuts, and seeds, releasing their nutrients.

The body quickly absorbs the resulting smooth and nutrient-rich mixture. Unlike traditional juicers that remove fiber, the Nutribullet retains the fiber content, ensuring a slower release of nutrients into the bloodstream and promoting satiety.

1.4 The Role of Nutrition in Healthy Living Nutrition is vital in maintaining overall health and well-being. A balanced and nutrient-rich diet provides Nutrients such as vitamins, minerals, antioxidants, and phytochemicals essential for supporting the immune system, preventing chronic diseases, and promoting energy levels.

This section explores the different types of nutrients and their bodily functions. In a well-rounded diet, we also discuss the importance of macronutrients (carbohydrates, proteins, and fats) and micronutrients (vitamins and minerals).

Furthermore, we delve into "eating the rainbow" and how consuming a diverse range of colorful fruits and vegetables ensures a broad spectrum of nutrients.

1.5 The Power of Whole Foods refers to foods in their natural, unprocessed state. These include fresh fruits, vegetables, nuts, seeds, whole grains, and legumes. Unlike processed foods that may contain added sugars, unhealthy fats, and artificial ingredients, whole foods provide essential nutrients without the added drawbacks.

This section explores the benefits of whole foods over processed foods and their impact on overall health. We discuss how whole foods are rich in vitamins, minerals, fiber, and antioxidants, all of which contribute to better digestion, improved immunity, and a reduced risk of chronic diseases.

The Nutribullet recipe book focuses on incorporating a variety of whole foods into Nutriblast recipes, making it easier for readers to enjoy the full spectrum of health benefits these ingredients offer.

1.6 Making Healthy Living a Habit Adopting a healthy lifestyle is not just about following a temporary diet; it's about making sustainable changes that become habits. This section provides practical tips and strategies for integrating healthy habits into daily life.

We discuss the importance of meal planning and preparation and how to make smart choices when eating out. Mindful eating practices are also explored, emphasizing the importance of paying attention to hunger cues and eating with intention.

Additionally, we address the challenges that may arise when trying to make healthy changes, such as dealing with cravings and managing stress. Strategies for staying motivated and accountable on the journey to a healthier lifestyle are also shared.

1.7 How This Book Can Help You As we progress through the Nutribullet recipe book, readers will discover many delicious and nutrient-packed recipes. The recipes are carefully curated to cater to various dietary preferences and health goals, ensuring something for everyone.

Each recipe is accompanied by a detailed list of ingredients and step-by-step instructions, making it easy to recreate the Nutriblasts at home. Nutritional information for each recipe is also provided, giving readers insight into the nutrient content of their creations.

This book aims to inspire and empower readers to take charge of their health by incorporating the Nutribullet and these wholesome recipes into their daily lives. By doing so, readers can journey towards improved energy, well-being, and overall vitality.

Serves as a comprehensive introduction to the Nutribullet and its role in healthy living. Readers are acquainted with the benefits of the Nutribullet, its extraction technology, and the vast range of nutrients it can unlock from whole foods. Understanding the significance of nutrition and whole foods paves the way for readers to embrace a more health-conscious lifestyle. The chapter also provides practical tips for making healthy habits sustainable, ensuring readers have the tools they need for a successful health journey. Throughout the Nutribullet recipe book, readers will discover many delicious and nutrient-dense recipes, further supporting their quest for better health and vitality.

ENERGIZING BREAKFAST BLENDS:

SUNRISE CITRUS BURST:

INGREDIENTS:

- One large orange, peeled and segmented
- 1 cup of pineapple chunks
- One medium carrot, peeled and chopped
- 1/2 inch fresh ginger, peeled and grated
- 1 cup of coconut water or water
- Ice cubes (optional)

INSTRUCTIONS:

1. Place all the ingredients in a blender.
2. Blend until smooth and creamy.
3. If desired, add ice cubes and blend again for a colder consistency.
4. Pour into a glass and enjoy the refreshing Sunrise Citrus Burst smoothie!

BANANA BERRY BLAST:

INGREDIENTS:

- Two ripe bananas
- 1 cup of mixed berries (strawberries, blueberries, raspberries)
- 1 cup of plain yogurt or almond milk (for a vegan option)
- One tbsp of honey or maple syrup (optional for added sweetness)
- Ice cubes (optional)

INSTRUCTIONS:

1. Peel the bananas and place them in a blender.
2. Add the mixed berries, yogurt or almond milk, and honey/maple syrup (if using).
3. Blend until smooth and creamy.
4. Add some ice cubes and blend again if you prefer a colder smoothie.
5. Pour into a glass and enjoy the delicious Banana Berry Blast!

OATMEAL COOKIE SMOOTHIE:

INGREDIENTS:

- 1 cup of rolled oats
- One ripe banana
- One tbsp of almond butter or peanut butter
- 1 cup of milk (dairy or plant-based)
- 1/2 tsp ground cinnamon
- 1/4 tsp vanilla extract
- Ice cubes (optional)

INSTRUCTIONS:

1. Combine the rolled oats, ripe banana, almond butter, milk, ground cinnamon, and vanilla extract in a blender.
2. Blend until all the ingredients are well combined, and the mixture is smooth.
3. Add some ice cubes and blend again for a colder and creamier smoothie.
4. Pour into a glass and enjoy the comforting Oatmeal Cookie Smoothie!

TROPICAL TURMERIC DELIGHT:

INGREDIENTS:

- 1 cup of chopped mango
- 1/2 cup of pineapple chunks
- One medium banana
- 1/2 tsp ground turmeric
- One tbsp of chia seeds
- 1 cup of coconut water or orange juice
- Ice cubes (optional)

INSTRUCTIONS:

1. Place the mango, pineapple, banana, ground turmeric, chia seeds, and coconut water/orange juice in a blender.
2. Blend until all the ingredients are thoroughly mixed, and the smoothie is creamy.
3. Add some ice cubes and blend again for a more excellent smoothie if desired.
4. Pour into a glass and enjoy the Tropical Turmeric Delight!

GREEN ENERGY BOOSTER:

INGREDIENTS:

- 2 cups of fresh spinach
- One medium cucumber peeled and chopped
- One green apple, cored and chopped
- 1/2 lemon, juiced
- One tbsp of fresh parsley or cilantro
- 1 cup of coconut water or water
- Ice cubes (optional)

INSTRUCTIONS:

1. Place the fresh spinach, chopped cucumber, green apple, lemon juice, parsley/cilantro, and coconut water/water in a blender.

2. Blend until the mixture is smooth and all the ingredients are well combined.
3. You can add some ice cubes and blend again for an excellent smoothie.
4. Pour into a glass and enjoy the nutritious Green Energy Booster!

ALMOND DATE BREAKFAST SHAKE:

INGREDIENTS:

- 1 cup of almond milk
- One ripe banana
- 5-6 pitted dates
- Two tbsp of almond butter
- 1/2 tsp vanilla extract
- 1/4 tsp ground cinnamon
- 1/4 cup of rolled oats
- Ice cubes (optional)

INSTRUCTIONS:

1. Combine almond milk, ripe banana, pitted dates, almond
2. Add the rolled oats to the blender for extra fiber and thickness.
3. Blend all the ingredients until smooth and creamy.
4. Add a few ice cubes and blend again for a refreshing chill if desired.
5. Pour the Almond Date Breakfast Shake into a glass and enjoy!

PEANUT BUTTER BANANA POWER SMOOTHIE:

INGREDIENTS:

- 1 cup of milk (dairy or plant-based)
- Two ripe bananas
- Two tbsp of peanut butter
- One tbsp of honey or maple syrup (optional for added sweetness)
- 1/2 tsp chia seeds (optional)
- 1/2 tsp ground flaxseed (optional)
- Ice cubes (optional)

INSTRUCTIONS:

1. In a blender, combine milk, ripe bananas, peanut butter, and honey/maple syrup (if using).
2. Add chia seeds and ground flaxseed to boost the nutritional content if desired.
3. Blend all the ingredients until smooth and creamy.
4. You can add some ice cubes and blend for a colder smoothie.
5. Pour the Peanut Butter Banana Power Smoothie into a glass and enjoy the energizing flavors!

MANGO COCONUT MORNING BLISS:

INGREDIENTS:

- 1 cup of coconut milk
- One ripe mango peeled and pitted
- 1/2 cup of plain Greek yogurt
- One tbsp of honey or agave syrup (adjust to taste)
- 1/2 tsp grated fresh ginger
- 1/4 cup of shredded coconut (optional)
- Ice cubes (optional)

INSTRUCTIONS:

1. Combine coconut milk, ripe mango, Greek yogurt, honey/agave syrup, and grated ginger in a blender.
2. Add shredded coconut to the blender if you want a more coconutty flavor.
3. Blend all the ingredients until the mixture is smooth and creamy.
4. Add some ice cubes and blend again if you prefer a colder smoothie.
5. Pour the Mango Coconut Morning Bliss into a glass and enjoy the tropical delight!

BLUEBERRY SPINACH SUPERCHARGE:

INGREDIENTS:

- 1 cup of almond milk
- 1 cup of fresh or fr0uncesen blueberries
- 1 cup of fresh spinach leaves
- One ripe banana
- One tbsp of almond butter
- One tbsp of honey or maple syrup (optional for added sweetness)
- Ice cubes (optional)

INSTRUCTIONS:

1. In a blender, combine almond milk, blueberries, fresh spinach, ripe banana, almond butter, and honey/maple syrup (if using).
2. Blend all the ingredients until the mixture turns vibrant purple and has a smooth texture.

3. Add some ice cubes and blend again if you like a colder smoothie.
4. Pour the Blueberry Spinach Supercharge into a glass and enjoy the antioxidant-rich goodness!

COFFEE LOVER'S WAKE-UP CALL:

INGREDIENTS:

- 1 cup of brewed coffee, cooled
- 1 cup of milk (dairy or plant-based)
- One ripe banana
- One tbsp of almond butter or peanut butter
- One tbsp of honey or sweetener of your choice (optional)
- Ice cubes (optional)

INSTRUCTIONS:

1. In a blender, combine brewed coffee (ensure it's cooled), milk, ripe banana, almond butter/peanut butter, and honey/sweetener (if using).
2. Blend all the ingredients until the mixture is well combined and frothy.
3. Add some ice cubes and blend again for a colder and creamier texture.
4. Pour the Coffee Lover's Wake-Up Call into a glass and savor the coffee-infused goodness!

REFRESHING SMOOTHIE BOWLS:

ACAI BERRY BOWL WITH GRANOLA CRUNCH:

INGREDIENTS:

- Two packs of frOuncesen acai berry puree (unsweetened)
- One ripe banana
- 1/2 cup of frOuncesen mixed berries (blueberries, strawberries, raspberries)
- 1/4 cup of almond milk (or any other plant-based milk)
- One tbsp of honey or maple syrup (optional for added sweetness)
- Fresh berries (blueberries, strawberries, raspberries) for topping
- Granola for crunch
- Chia seeds for extra nutrition

INSTRUCTIONS:

1. Combine the frOuncesen acai berry puree, ripe banana, frOuncesen mixed berries, and almond milk in a blender.
2. Blend until you achieve a smooth and creamy texture. If needed, add a bit more almond milk to help with blending.
3. Taste the mixture and add honey or maple syrup if you desire extra sweetness. Blend again to incorporate.
4. Pour the acai berry mixture into a bowl.
5. For added crunch and nutrition, top with fresh berries, granola, and chia seeds.
6. Serve immediately and enjoy your Acai Berry Bowl!

GREEN GODDESS BOWL WITH KIWI AND CHIA SEEDS:

INGREDIENTS:

- 2 cups of baby spinach
- One ripe avocado
- One ripe kiwi, peeled and sliced

- 1/2 cucumber, peeled and sliced
- 1/2 cup of pineapple chunks
- One tbsp of chia seeds
- 1/4 cup of coconut water (or any other liquid of your choice)

INSTRUCTIONS:

1. Combine the baby spinach, ripe avocado, kiwi, cucumber, and pineapple chunks in a blender.
2. Add the coconut water to help with blending and achieve your preferred consistency.
3. Blend until the mixture becomes smooth and creamy.
4. Pour the green goddess mixture into a bowl.
5. Top with sliced kiwi and sprinkle chia seeds for added texture and nutrition.
6. Serve immediately and enjoy your Green Goddess Bowl!

DRAGON FRUIT DELIGHT BOWL:

INGREDIENTS:

- One dragon fruit, peeled and diced
- 1/2 cup of fr0uncesen mango chunks
- 1/2 cup of fr0uncesen pineapple chunks
- 1/4 cup of coconut milk
- 1 tbsp honey or agave syrup (optional for sweetness)
- Sliced banana, kiwi, or other fruits for topping
- Shredded coconut for garnish

INSTRUCTIONS:

1. Combine the diced dragon fruit, fr0uncesen mango chunks, and a blender.

2. Blend until you achieve a smooth and vibrant pink mixture.
3. Taste the variety and add honey or agave syrup if you prefer it sweeter. Blend again to incorporate.
4. Pour the dragon fruit delight mixture into a bowl.
5. Top with sliced banana, kiwi, or any other fruits you like, and sprinkle shredded coconut for garnish.
6. Serve immediately and enjoy your Dragon Fruit Delight Bowl!

RASPBERRY COCONUT BLISS BOWL:

INGREDIENTS:

- 1 cup of frOuncesen raspberries
- One ripe banana
- 1/2 cup of coconut milk
- One tbsp of almond butter or coconut butter
- One tbsp of honey or maple syrup (optional for added sweetness)
- Fresh raspberries for topping
- Coconut flakes for garnish

INSTRUCTIONS:

1. Combine the frOuncesen raspberries, ripe bananas, coconut milk, and almond butter in a blender.
2. Blend until the mixture becomes smooth and creamy.
3. Taste the variety and add honey or maple syrup if you desire extra sweetness. Blend again to incorporate.
4. Pour the raspberry-coconut bliss mixture into a bowl.
5. Top with fresh raspberries and sprinkle coconut flakes on top for garnish.

6. Serve immediately and enjoy your Raspberry Coconut Bliss Bowl!

TROPICAL MANGO-PINEAPPLE PARADISE BOWL:

INGREDIENTS:

- One ripe mango, peeled and diced
- 1 cup of frOuncesen pineapple chunks
- 1/2 cup of orange juice
- 1/4 cup of Greek yogurt (or any plant-based yogurt for a vegan option)
- One tbsp of shredded coconut
- Sliced kiwi or other tropical fruits for topping

INSTRUCTIONS:

1. Combine the diced ripe mango, frOuncesen pineapple chunks, orange juice, and Greek yogurt in a blender.
2. Blend until you achieve a smooth and tropical-flavored mixture.
3. Pour the tropical mango-pineapple paradise mixture into a bowl.
4. Top with sliced kiwi or other tropical fruits of your choice, and sprinkle shredded coconut on top for added flavor.
5. Serve immediately and enjoy your Tropical Mango-Pineapple Paradise Bowl!

BERRY BLAST SMOOTHIE BOWL WITH ALMONDS:

INGREDIENTS:

- 1 cup of fr0uncesen mixed berries (blueberries, strawberries, raspberries)
- One ripe banana
- 1/2 cup of Greek yogurt (or any plant-based yogurt for a vegan option)
- 1/4 cup of almond milk (or any other milk of your choice)
- One tbsp of honey or maple syrup (optional for added sweetness)
- Fresh berries (blueberries, strawberries, raspberries) for topping
- Sliced almonds for crunch

INSTRUCTIONS:

1. Combine the fr0uncesen mixed berries, ripe banana, Greek yogurt, and almond milk in a blender.
2. Blend until you achieve a smooth and creamy texture.
3. Taste the mixture and add honey or maple syrup if you prefer it sweeter. Blend again to incorporate.
4. Pour the berry blast smoothie mixture into a bowl.
5. Top with fresh berries and sprinkle sliced almonds on top for added crunch.
6. Serve immediately and enjoy your Berry Blast Smoothie Bowl with Almonds!

KIWI-BANANA SMOOTHIE BOWL WITH FLAX SEEDS:

INGREDIENTS:

- Two ripe kiwis, peeled and diced
- One ripe banana
- 1/2 cup of spinach leaves (optional, for added nutrients)

- 1/4 cup of coconut water (or any other liquid of your choice)
- One tbsp of flax seeds
- Sliced kiwi, banana, or other fruits for topping
- Coconut flakes for garnish

INSTRUCTIONS:

1. Combine the diced ripe kiwis, ripe banana, spinach leaves, and coconut water in a blender.
2. Blend until the mixture becomes smooth and creamy.
3. Add flax seeds to the mixture and blend again briefly to mix them in.
4. Pour the kiwi-banana smoothie mixture into a bowl.
5. Top with sliced kiwi, banana, or any other fruits you like, and sprinkle coconut flakes for added flavor.
6. Serve immediately and enjoy your Kiwi-Banana Smoothie Bowl with Flax Seeds!

PITAYA (DRAGON FRUIT) AND BANANA BOWL:

INGREDIENTS:

- One ripe pitaya (dragon fruit), peeled and diced
- One ripe banana
- 1/2 cup of frOuncesen mango chunks
- 1/4 cup of coconut milk (or any other milk of your choice)
- One tbsp of chia seeds
- Fresh pitaya (dragon fruit) cubes for topping
- Granola for crunch

INSTRUCTIONS:

1. Combine the diced pitaya (dragon fruit), ripe banana, frOuncesen mango chunks, and coconut milk in a blender.
2. Blend until the mixture becomes smooth and vibrant in color.
3. Add chia seeds to the mixture and blend briefly to mix them in.
4. Pour the pitaya and banana smoothie mixture into a bowl.
5. Top with fresh pitaya (dragon fruit) cubes, and sprinkle granola for added crunch.
6. Serve immediately, and enjoy your Pitaya (Dragon Fruit) and Banana Bowl!

PEANUT BUTTER CHOCOLATE SMOOTHIE BOWL:

INGREDIENTS:

- Two ripe bananas
- Two tbsp of peanut butter
- One tbsp of cocoa powder
- 1/2 cup of almond milk (or any other milk of your choice)
- One tbsp of honey or maple syrup (optional for added sweetness)
- Sliced bananas, chopped peanuts, and chocolate chips for topping

INSTRUCTIONS:

1. Combine the ripe bananas, peanut butter, cocoa powder, and almond milk in a blender.
2. Blend until the mixture becomes smooth and creamy with a chocolate-peanut butter flavor.
3. Taste the variety and add honey or maple syrup if you prefer it sweeter. Blend again to incorporate.

4. Pour the peanut butter chocolate smoothie mixture into a bowl.
5. Top with sliced bananas, chopped peanuts, and chocolate chips for added texture and taste.
6. Serve immediately and enjoy your Peanut Butter Chocolate Smoothie Bowl!

GREEN TEA AND BERRY BLAST BOWL:

INGREDIENTS:

- 1 cup of fr0uncesen mixed berries (blueberries, strawberries, raspberries)
- One ripe banana
- 1/2 cup of brewed green tea, cooled
- 1/4 cup of Greek yogurt (or any plant-based yogurt for a vegan option)
- One tbsp of honey or agave syrup (optional for sweetness)
- Fresh berries (blueberries, strawberries, raspberries) for topping
- Hemp seeds for garnish

INSTRUCTIONS:

1. Combine the fr0uncesen mixed berries, ripe banana, brewed green tea, and Greek yogurt in a blender.
2. Blend until you achieve a smooth and creamy texture.
3. Taste the mixture and add honey or agave syrup if you desire extra sweetness. Blend again to incorporate.
4. Pour the green tea and berry blast smoothie mixture into a bowl.
5. Top with fresh berries and sprinkle hemp seeds for added nutrition and texture.

6. Serve immediately and enjoy your Green Tea and Berry Blast Bowl!

NUTRIENT-PACKED GREEN SMOOTHIES:

KALE-PINEAPPLE GREEN REVIVER:

INGREDIENTS:

- 2 cups of kale leaves (stems removed)
- 1 cup of pineapple chunks (fresh or fr0uncesen)
- 1 cup of coconut water
- One tbsp of honey or maple syrup (optional for sweetness)

INSTRUCTIONS:

1. Wash the kale leaves thoroughly and remove the tough stems.
2. In a blender, combine kale, pineapple chunks, and coconut water.
3. Blend until smooth.
4. Taste the mixture and add honey or maple syrup if you prefer a sweeter taste.
5. Pour into glasses and serve chilled.

CUCUMBER MINT GREEN REFRESHER:

INGREDIENTS:

- Two medium cucumbers (peeled and chopped)
- 1/4 cup of fresh mint leaves

- Juice of 1 lime
- 2 cups of water
- Ice cubes

INSTRUCTIONS:

1. Place the chopped cucumbers, mint leaves, and lime juice in a blender.
2. Add water and blend until smooth.
3. Strain the mixture through a fine-mesh sieve if you prefer a smoother texture.
4. Serve over ice and garnish with a mint sprig.

SPINACH AVOCADO DREAM:

INGREDIENTS:

- 2 cups of fresh spinach leaves
- One ripe avocado (peeled and pitted)
- One banana
- 1 cup of almond milk (or any plant-based milk of your choice)
- One tbsp of honey or agave syrup (optional for sweetness)

INSTRUCTIONS:

1. Combine spinach, avocado, banana, and almond milk in a blender.
2. Blend until creamy and smooth.
3. Taste the mixture and add honey or agave syrup if you prefer it sweeter.
4. Pour into glasses and enjoy this nutritious green smoothie.

DETOXIFYING GREEN ELIXIR:

INGREDIENTS:

- 1 cup of fresh spinach leaves
- One green apple (cored and chopped)
- One stalk of celery (chopped)
- 1/2 cucumber (peeled and chopped)
- 1-inch piece of ginger (peeled)
- Juice of 1 lemon
- 1 cup of water

INSTRUCTIONS:

1. Put spinach, green apple, celery, cucumber, ginger, and lemon juice in a blender.
2. Add water and blend until everything is well combined.
3. Strain the mixture through a fine-mesh sieve if you prefer a smoother texture.
4. Serve over ice and enjoy this refreshing detox drink.

ZESTY GREEN GINGERADE:

INGREDIENTS:

- 2 cups of baby spinach
- 1-inch piece of fresh ginger (peeled)
- Juice of 2 lemons
- One tbsp of honey or maple syrup (optional for sweetness)
- 2 cups of water
- Pinch of cayenne pepper (optional for added spice)

INSTRUCTIONS:

1. Combine baby spinach, ginger, lemon juice, and water in a blender.
2. Blend until smooth.
3. Taste the mixture and add honey or maple syrup for sweetness if desired.
4. Add a pinch of cayenne pepper for a zesty kick.
5. Serve chilled, and enjoy this invigorating green gingerade.

GREEN GRAPES AND HONEYDEW MELON BLEND:

INGREDIENTS:

- 2 cups of green grapes
- 2 cups of honeydew melon (cubed)
- 1 cup of coconut water
- Ice cubes (optional)

INSTRUCTIONS:

1. Wash the green grapes and remove any stems.
2. Combine green grapes, honeydew melon, and coconut water in a blender.
3. Blend until smooth.
4. If desired, add ice cubes and blend again for a colder drink.
5. Pour into glasses and enjoy this refreshing green grape and honeydew melon blend.

KIWI-KALE SUPER GREENS SMOOTHIE:

INGREDIENTS:

- Two ripe kiwis (peeled and chopped)
- 1 cup of kale leaves (stems removed)

- One ripe banana
- 1 cup of almond milk (or any plant-based milk of your choice)
- One tbsp of chia seeds (optional for added nutrition)

INSTRUCTIONS:

1. Combine kiwis, kale, banana, and almond milk in a blender.
2. Blend until creamy and smooth.
3. Add chia seeds for extra nutritional benefits and blend again briefly.
4. Pour into glasses and enjoy this super greens smoothie with vitamins and minerals.

GREEN GODDESS PROTEIN SHAKE:

INGREDIENTS:

- 1 cup of baby spinach
- 1/2 avocado (peeled and pitted)
- One scoop of plant-based protein powder (such as pea or hemp protein)
- One tbsp of almond butter
- 1 cup of almond milk (or any plant-based milk of your choice)
- One tsp of honey or maple syrup (optional for sweetness)

INSTRUCTIONS:

1. Combine baby spinach, avocado, protein powder, almond butter, and almond milk in a blender.
2. Blend until smooth and creamy.
3. Taste the mixture and add honey or maple syrup if you prefer it sweeter.

4. Pour into glasses and enjoy this nutrient-packed green goddess protein shake.

BROCCOLI-APPLE GREEN DELIGHT:

INGREDIENTS:

- 1 cup of broccoli florets
- One green apple (cored and chopped)
- 1/2 cup of cucumber (peeled and chopped)
- 1 cup of water or coconut water
- Juice of 1 lime
- Ice cubes

INSTRUCTIONS:

1. Steam the broccoli florets until tender and let them cool.
2. Combine steamed broccoli, green apple, cucumber, water, and lime juice in a blender.
3. Blend until smooth.
4. If desired, add ice cubes and blend again for a chilled drink.
5. Pour into glasses and enjoy this delicious and nutritious green delight.

MINTY GREEN WATERMELON COOLER:

INGREDIENTS:

- 2 cups of diced seedless watermelon
- 1 cup of cucumber (peeled and chopped)
- 1/4 cup of fresh mint leaves
- Juice of 1 lime
- 1 cup of coconut water
- Ice cubes

INSTRUCTIONS:

1. Combine diced watermelon, cucumber, mint leaves, lime juice, and coconut water in a blender.
2. Blend until smooth.
3. Add ice cubes and blend again for a more relaxed drink if desired.
4. Pour into glasses and enjoy this refreshing minty green watermelon cooler.

IMMUNITY BOOSTING BLENDS:

CITRUS IMMUNE DEFENDER:

INGREDIENTS:

- One medium orange, peeled and segmented
- One medium grapefruit, peeled and segmented
- One lemon, juiced
- One tbsp honey (optional)
- 1 cup of water
- Ice cubes

INSTRUCTIONS:

1. In a blender, combine the orange segments, grapefruit segments, lemon juice, honey (if using), and water.
2. Blend until smooth and well combined.
3. Pour the mixture into a glass filled with ice cubes.
4. Enjoy the refreshing and immune-boosting Citrus Immune Defender!

GINGER-TURMERIC ANTIOXIDANT BLAST:

INGREDIENTS:

- 1-inch fresh ginger, peeled and chopped
- One tsp of ground turmeric
- One tbsp honey (optional)
- 1 cup of coconut water or plain water
- Ice cubes

INSTRUCTIONS:

1. Add the chopped ginger, ground turmeric, honey (if using), and coconut water (or plain water) in a blender.
2. Blend until the ingredients are well combined, and the ginger is fully incorporated.
3. Pour the mixture into a glass filled with ice cubes.
4. Sip on this Ginger-Turmeric Antioxidant Blast to support your immune system and benefit from its anti-inflammatory properties.

BERRY ANTIVIRAL BOOSTER:

INGREDIENTS:

- 1 cup of mixed berries (such as strawberries, blueberries, and raspberries)
- One tbsp of fresh lemon juice
- One tbsp honey (optional)
- 1 cup of almond milk or any plant-based milk
- Ice cubes

INSTRUCTIONS:

1. Add mixed berries, fresh lemon juice, honey (if using), and almond milk (or your preferred plant-based milk) in a blender.

2. Blend until the mixture is smooth and creamy.
3. Pour the berry booster into a glass filled with ice cubes.
4. Savor the delicious Berry Antiviral Booster to fortify your immune system with antioxidants.

PINEAPPLE-ORANGE COLD BUSTER:

INGREDIENTS:

- 1 cup of fresh pineapple chunks
- One medium orange, peeled and segmented
- One tbsp of raw honey (optional)
- 1/2 cup of coconut water or plain water
- Ice cubes

INSTRUCTIONS:

1. Combine the fresh pineapple chunks, orange segments, raw honey (if using), and coconut water (or plain water) in a blender.
2. Blend until all the ingredients are thoroughly mixed.
3. Pour the pineapple-orange elixir into a glass filled with ice cubes.
4. Drink up this Pineapple-Orange Cold Buster to strengthen your immune system and ward off colds.

ELDERBERRY AND BLUEBERRY IMMUNE ELIXIR:

INGREDIENTS:

- 1/2 cup of fresh or fr0uncesen blueberries
- One tbsp of elderberry syrup or concentrate
- 1 cup of plain yogurt or dairy-free yogurt
- One tbsp of chia seeds (optional)

- Ice cubes

INSTRUCTIONS:

1. In a blender, add the blueberries, elderberry syrup or concentrate, plain yogurt (or dairy-free yogurt), and chia seeds (if using).
2. Blend until you achieve a smooth and creamy consistency.
3. Pour the elixir into a glass filled with ice cubes.
4. Relish this Elderberry and Blueberry Immune Elixir to support your immune system and benefit from the rich antioxidants.

CARROT-GINGER IMMUNITY BLEND:

INGREDIENTS:

- Two large carrots, peeled and chopped
- 1-inch piece of fresh ginger peeled and chopped
- 1 cup of water
- One tbsp honey (optional for sweetness)

INSTRUCTIONS:

1. In a blender, combine the chopped carrots, ginger, and water. Blend until you get a smooth consistency.
2. If you prefer a sweeter taste, add honey and blend again.
3. Pour into a glass and enjoy your Carrot-Ginger Immunity Blend!

GREEN APPLE-ECHINACEA BOOST:

INGREDIENTS:

- Two medium green apples, cored and chopped

- One tsp dried Echinacea herb (or 1 Echinacea tea bag)
- 1 cup of water
- 1/2 lemon, juiced

INSTRUCTIONS:

a. In a saucepan, bring the water to a boil and add the Echinacea herb (or tea bag). Let it steep for 5 minutes. b. In a blender, combine the chopped green apples and lemon juice. c. Strain the Echinacea tea into the blender with the apples and lemon juice. d. Blend until smooth. e. Pour into a glass and enjoy your Green Apple-Echinacea Boost!

Beetroot-Orange Immune Supporter:

INGREDIENTS:

One medium beetroot, peeled and chopped

Two medium oranges, peeled and segmented

1/2 cup of water

One tbsp of chia seeds (optional for added nutrients)

INSTRUCTIONS: a. Combine the chopped beetroot, orange segments, and water in a blender. b. Blend until smooth. c. Add chia seeds and blend for a few more seconds to incorporate them if desired. d. Pour into a glass and enjoy your Beetroot-Orange Immune Supporter!

Spinach-Grapefruit Vitamin C Blast:

INGREDIENTS:

2 cups of fresh spinach leaves

One large grapefruit, peeled and segmented

1/2 cup of coconut water (or regular water)

INSTRUCTIONS: a. Combine the fresh spinach leaves, grapefruit segments, and coconut water in a blender. b. Blend until smooth. c. Pour into a glass and enjoy your Spinach-Grapefruit Vitamin C Blast!

Garlic-Honey Flu Fighter:

INGREDIENTS:

3-4 garlic cloves, peeled

One tbsp of raw honey

1 cup of warm water

Juice of 1/2 lemon (optional, for extra Vitamin C)

INSTRUCTIONS:

1. In a blender, combine the peeled garlic cloves and warm water.
2. Blend until the garlic is thoroughly mixed with the water.
3. Pour the mixture through a fine mesh strainer to separate the liquid from any garlic pieces.
4. Stir in the raw honey and lemon juice (if using) into the garlic water
5. Pour into a glass and enjoy your Garlic-Honey Flu Fighter!

PROTEIN-PACKED POWER BLENDS:
ALMOND BUTTER BANANA PROTEIN SHAKE:

INGREDIENTS:

- One ripe banana
- Two tbsp of almond butter
- 1 cup of almond milk
- One scoop of vanilla protein powder
- One tsp of honey (optional)
- Ice cubes (optional)

INSTRUCTIONS:

1. Peel and slice the ripe banana.
2. In a blender, combine the sliced banana, almond butter, almond milk, vanilla protein powder, and honey (if using).
3. Blend until all the ingredients are well combined, and the shake is smooth.
4. Add some ice cubes and blend again if you prefer a colder shake.
5. Pour the shake into a glass and enjoy your Almond Butter Banana Protein Shake!

CHOCOLATE PEANUT BUTTER POWERHOUSE:

INGREDIENTS:

- 1 cup of milk (dairy or plant-based)
- One ripe banana
- Two tbsp of peanut butter
- One tbsp of cocoa powder
- One scoop of chocolate protein powder
- Ice cubes (optional)

INSTRUCTIONS:

1. Peel and slice the ripe banana.

2. Add the milk, sliced banana, peanut butter, cocoa powder, and chocolate protein powder in a blender.
3. Blend until all the ingredients are well combined, and the shake is creamy.
4. If you want a thicker or colder shake, add some ice cubes and blend again.
5. Pour the Chocolate Peanut Butter Powerhouse into a glass and enjoy!

CHIA SEED AND RASPBERRY PROTEIN BOOST:

INGREDIENTS:

- 1 cup of frOuncesen or fresh raspberries
- 1 cup of almond milk
- One scoop of vanilla protein powder
- One tbsp of chia seeds
- One tsp of honey (optional)

INSTRUCTIONS:

1. Combine the raspberries, almond milk, vanilla protein powder, chia seeds, and honey (if using).
2. Blend until the shake is smooth and the ingredients are well-mixed.
3. Pour the Chia Seed and Raspberry Protein Boost into a glass.
4. You can top it with some additional chia seeds or fresh raspberries.
5. Enjoy the protein-boosting goodness!

GREEK YOGURT BERRY BLAST:

INGREDIENTS:

- 1 cup of Greek yogurt
- 1/2 cup of mixed berries (blueberries, strawberries, raspberries)
- One tbsp honey
- One scoop of vanilla protein powder
- 1/4 cup of milk (dairy or plant-based)

INSTRUCTIONS:

1. Add Greek yogurt, mixed berries, honey, vanilla protein powder, and milk in a blender.
2. Blend until all the ingredients are well combined, and the shake is creamy.
3. Taste and adjust sweetness with more honey if desired.
4. Pour the Greek Yogurt Berry Blast into a glass and enjoy!

HEMP SEED PROTEIN PARADISE:

INGREDIENTS:

- 1 cup of coconut milk (or any other milk of your choice)
- One ripe banana
- Two tbsp hemp seeds
- One scoop of vanilla protein powder
- One tbsp of almond butter
- Ice cubes (optional)

INSTRUCTIONS:

1. Peel and slice the ripe banana.
2. Combine the coconut milk, sliced banana, hemp seeds, vanilla protein powder, and almond butter in a blender.
3. Blend until all the ingredients are well combined, and the shake is smooth.

4. Add some ice cubes and blend again if you want a colder shake.
5. Pour the Hemp Seed Protein Paradise into a glass and enjoy!

VANILLA COCONUT PROTEIN SMOOTHIE:

INGREDIENTS:

- 1 cup of coconut milk
- One scoop of vanilla protein powder
- One ripe banana
- One tbsp of almond butter
- 1/4 cup of shredded coconut
- Ice cubes (optional)

INSTRUCTIONS:

1. Add coconut milk, vanilla protein powder, ripe banana, almond butter, and shredded coconut in a blender.
2. Blend until smooth and creamy. Add some ice cubes and blend again if you prefer a colder smoothie.
3. Pour into a glass and enjoy your delicious Vanilla Coconut Protein Smoothie!

SPIRULINA PROTEIN POWER PUNCH:

INGREDIENTS:

- 1 cup of unsweetened almond milk
- One scoop of plant-based protein powder (unflavored or vanilla)
- One tsp of spirulina powder
- One tbsp of chia seeds

- 1/2 cup of frOuncesen mixed berries (blueberries, raspberries, strawberries)
- One tbsp of honey or maple syrup (optional for sweetness)

INSTRUCTIONS:

1. Add the almond milk, protein powder, spirulina powder, chia seeds, frOuncesen mixed berries, and honey/maple syrup (if using) to a blender.
2. Blend until the ingredients are well combined, and the smoothie is creamy.
3. Pour into a glass and enjoy your Spirulina Protein Power Punch!

QUINOA-BERRY PROTEIN SHAKE:

INGREDIENTS:

- 1 cup of unsweetened soy milk (or any milk of your choice)
- 1/2 cup of cooked quinoa, cooled
- 1/2 cup of mixed berries (strawberries, blueberries, raspberries)
- One tbsp of almond butter
- One tbsp of honey or agave syrup (adjust to taste)
- A dash of cinnamon (optional)

INSTRUCTIONS:

1. In a blender, combine the soy milk, cooked quinoa, mixed berries, almond butter, honey/agave syrup, and cinnamon (if using).
2. Blend until smooth and all the ingredients are fully incorporated.

3. Pour into a glass and enjoy your nutritious Quinoa-Berry Protein Shake!

PUMPKIN SEED PROTEIN ELIXIR:

INGREDIENTS:

- 1 cup of unsweetened coconut water
- One scoop of pumpkin seed protein powder
- 1/2 cup of canned pumpkin puree
- One small ripe banana
- 1/2 tsp ground cinnamon
- 1/4 tsp ground nutmeg
- Ice cubes (optional)

INSTRUCTIONS:

1. Add coconut water, pumpkin seed protein powder, canned pumpkin puree, ripe banana, ground cinnamon, and ground nutmeg in a blender.
2. Blend until all the ingredients are well combined, and the smoothie is creamy.
3. Add some ice cubes and blend again for a colder texture if desired.
4. Pour into a glass and enjoy your Pumpkin Seed Protein Elixir!

SPINACH-TOFU PROTEIN SUPERCHARGE:

INGREDIENTS:

- 1 cup of unsweetened almond milk
- 1 cup of fresh spinach leaves
- 1/2 cup of silken tofu
- One ripe pear

- One tbsp of almond butter
- One tbsp of chia seeds
- One tsp of honey or maple syrup (adjust to taste)

INSTRUCTIONS:

1. Combine the almond milk, fresh spinach leaves, silken tofu, ripe pear, almond butter, chia seeds, and honey/maple syrup in a blender.
2. Blend until the ingredients are thoroughly mixed and the smoothie is creamy.
3. Pour into a glass and enjoy your nutrient-packed Spinach-Tofu Protein Supercharge!

SUPERFOOD ELIXIRS AND SHOTS:

TURMERIC-GINGER WELLNESS SHOT:

INGREDIENTS:

- 1-inch piece of fresh turmeric root peeled
- 1-inch piece of fresh ginger root peeled
- One small lemon, juiced
- 1/4 tsp black pepper
- 1/2 tsp honey (optional for sweetness)
- 1/2 cup of water

INSTRUCTIONS:

1. In a blender or juicer, add the peeled turmeric and ginger roots.
2. Add the lemon juice, black pepper, and honey (if using).
3. Pour in the water to help with blending.
4. Blend all the ingredients until smooth.

5. Strain the mixture using a fine mesh strainer to remove any pulp.
6. Pour the strained liquid into a small shot glass.
7. Drink the wellness shot immediately for a boost of immune-boosting and anti-inflammatory benefits.

WHEATGRASS AND LEMON DETOX ELIXIR:

INGREDIENTS:

- 1 ounce fresh wheatgrass (or wheatgrass powder)
- Juice of 1/2 lemon
- 1/2 cup of filtered water
- One tsp of honey (optional for sweetness)

INSTRUCTIONS:

1. If using fresh wheatgrass, wash it thoroughly to remove any dirt.
2. In a blender, add the wheatgrass and filtered water.
3. Blend until the wheatgrass is fully juiced and the mixture is smooth.
4. Strain the wheatgrass juice using a fine mesh strainer to remove any fibers.
5. Add the lemon juice and honey (if using) to the strained wheatgrass juice.
6. Stir well until the honey is dissolved.
7. Pour the detox elixir into a small glass and enjoy it immediately for a refreshing and detoxifying drink.

SPIRULINA ENERGIZING SHOT:

INGREDIENTS:

- One tsp of spirulina powder

- 1/2 cup of coconut water (or regular water)
- Juice of 1/2 lime
- 1/4 tsp honey (optional for sweetness)

INSTRUCTIONS:

1. In a small glass, add the spirulina powder and coconut water.
2. Squeeze in the lime juice.
3. Add honey, if using, to sweeten the shot.
4. Stir well until the spirulina is fully dissolved and the mixture is smooth.
5. Consume the energizing image immediately for a nutrient-packed, energizing boost.

MATCHA GREEN TEA ANTIOXIDANT ELIXIR:

INGREDIENTS:

- One tsp of matcha green tea powder
- 1/2 cup of hot water (not boiling, around 175°F/80°C)
- 1/4 cup of almond milk (or any milk of your choice)
- 1/2 tsp honey or maple syrup (optional for sweetness)

INSTRUCTIONS:

1. In a bowl, add the matcha green tea powder.
2. Pour the hot water over the matcha powder.
3. Whisk vigorously with bamboo or a small whisk until the matcha is fully dissolved and a frothy layer forms on top.
4. Heat the almond milk (or any milk) in a separate cup of and add the honey or maple syrup if desired.
5. Pour the matcha mixture into the milk and stir gently to combine.

6. Enjoy the antioxidant elixir while it's still warm to benefit from the goodness of matcha and its antioxidants.

CHIA SEED HYDRATION SHOT:

INGREDIENTS:

- One tbsp of chia seeds
- 1/2 cup of coconut water (or regular water)
- Juice of 1/2 orange
- 1/2 tsp agave syrup or honey (optional for sweetness)

INSTRUCTIONS:

1. In a small glass, combine the chia seeds and coconut water.
2. Stir well to prevent clumping and let it sit for about m a gel-like consistency.
3. Squeeze in the juice of half an orange.
4. Add agave syrup or honey if you prefer a sweeter taste.
5. Stir well until all ingredients are well mixed.
6. Consume the chia seed hydration shot immediately for a hydrating and refreshing experience.

ALOE VERA DIGESTIVE SOOTHER:

INGREDIENTS:

- 1 cup of fresh Aloe Vera gel (remove the green skin and scoop out the gel)
- 1/2 cup of water
- One tbsp of honey or maple syrup (optional)
- Juice of 1/2 lemon

INSTRUCTIONS:

1. In a blender, add the fresh Aloe Vera gel and water.
2. Blend on low speed until the mixture is well combined and smooth.
3. Add honey or maple syrup for sweetness and lemon juice for flavor if desired.
4. Blend again for a few seconds to incorporate the additional ingredients.
5. Pour the mixture into a glass and serve chilled. Enjoy the soothing benefits of Aloe Vera!

CACAO MACA MOOD BOOSTER:

INGREDIENTS:

- 1 cup of almond milk (or any plant-based milk of your choice)
- One tbsp of raw cacao powder
- One tsp of maca powder
- One tbsp of honey or agave syrup (adjust to taste)
- Pinch of sea salt

INSTRUCTIONS:

1. Heat the almond milk over medium heat in a small saucepan until it's warm but not boiling.
2. Add the cacao powder and maca powder to the warm almond milk.
3. Stir the mixture well until the powders are fully dissolved.
4. Add honey or agave syrup and a pinch of sea salt. Stir again to combine.
5. Pour the mood-boosting drink into a mug and savor its rich flavor.

GOJI BERRY BEAUTY ELIXIR:

INGREDIENTS:

- 1 cup of coconut water
- 1/4 cup of dried goji berries
- One tbsp of chia seeds
- 1/2 tsp grated fresh ginger
- One tsp of raw honey or maple syrup (optional)

INSTRUCTIONS:

1. Combine coconut water and dried goji berries in a glass jar or bottle.
2. Add chia seeds and grated ginger to the mixture.
3. If desired, sweeten with raw honey or maple syrup for added taste.
4. Ingredients.
5. Let the mixture sit in the refrigerator for at least 1-2 hours to allow the flavors to infuse.
6. Shake the elixir again before serving. Pour it into a glass and enjoy the beauty-boosting benefits of goji berries.

CAMU CAMU VITAMIN C SHOT:

INGREDIENTS:

- One tbsp Camu Camu powder
- 1/2 cup of water
- One tbsp of honey or agave syrup (optional)

INSTRUCTIONS:

1. In a small glass, add Camu Camu powder and water.
2. Stir well until the powder is fully dissolved.
3. If desired, sweeten with honey or agave syrup.

4. Drink the vitamin C shot immediately to get a boost of natural vitamin C from Camu Camu.

MORINGA MINT DETOX SHOT:

INGREDIENTS:

- One tbsp of moringa powder
- 1/2 cup of coconut water
- Handful of fresh mint leaves
- Juice of 1/2 lime
- One tsp of raw honey or maple syrup (optional)

INSTRUCTIONS:

1. Combine moringa powder, coconut water, fresh mint leaves, and lime juice in a blender.
2. Blend until all the ingredients are well combined.
3. If desired, add honey or maple syrup for sweetness.
4. Blend again for a few seconds to incorporate the sweetener.
5. Pour the detox shot into a small glass and enjoy the refreshing and detoxifying effects.

NUTRIBULLET NUT BUTTER CREATIONS:

CLASSIC HOMEMADE ALMOND BUTTER:

INGREDIENTS:

- 2 cups of raw almonds

- 1/2 tsp salt (optional)

INSTRUCTIONS:

1. Preheat your oven to 350°F (175°C).
2. Spread the almonds evenly on a baking sheet and roast them in the oven for 10-12 minutes or until they become fragrant and slightly golden. Keep an eye on them to avoid burning.
3. Let the almonds cool for a few minutes.
4. Transfer the roasted almonds to a food processor or high-speed blender.
5. Blend the almonds on medium-high speed, occasionally scraping down the sides of the container. It may take some time, but eventually, the almonds will release their natural oils and turn into creamy almond butter.
6. Add a pinch of salt for flavor and continue blending until smooth.
7. Transfer the almond butter to a clean for a few weeks.

CINNAMON-VANILLA CASHEW BUTTER:

INGREDIENTS:

- 2 cups of raw cashews
- Two tbsp of maple syrup or honey
- One tsp of ground cinnamon
- One tsp of vanilla extract
- 1/4 tsp salt (optional)

INSTRUCTIONS:

1. Preheat your oven to 350°F (175°C).

2. Spread the cashews evenly on a baking sheet and roast them in the oven for 10-12 minutes or until they become lightly golden.
3. Let the cashews cool for a few minutes.
4. Transfer the roasted cashews to a food processor or high-speed blender.
5. Add the maple syrup or honey, ground cinnamon, vanilla extract, and salt (if using).
6. Blend the mixture on medium-high speed, occasionally scraping down the sides of the container. It may take some time, but the cashews eventually break into creamy butter.
7. Taste and adjust sweetness and cinnamon according to your preference.
8. Transfer the cinnamon-vanilla cashew butter for a few weeks.

MAPLE-PECAN BUTTER BLISS:

INGREDIENTS:

- 2 cups of raw pecans
- Two tbsp of maple syrup
- 1/4 tsp salt (optional)

INSTRUCTIONS:

1. Preheat your oven to 350°F (175°C).
2. Spread the pecans evenly on a baking sheet and roast them in the oven for about 8-10 minutes or until they become aromatic and lightly toasted.
3. Let the pecans cool for a few minutes.
4. Transfer the roasted pecans to a food processor or high-speed blender.

5. Add the maple syrup and salt (if using).
6. Blend the mixture on medium-high speed, occasionally scraping down the sides of the container. The pecans will gradually transform into creamy pecan butter.
7. Taste and add more maple syrup or salt if desired.
8. Transfer the maple-pecan butter bliss to a clean, airtight jar, and store it in the refrigerator for up to a few weeks.

CHOCOLATE-HAZELNUT INDULGENCE:

INGREDIENTS:

- 2 cups of raw hazelnuts
- Three tbsp cocoa powder
- Three tbsp powdered sugar or sweetener of your choice
- 1/4 tsp vanilla extract
- 1/4 tsp salt (optional)

INSTRUCTIONS:

1. Preheat your oven to 350°F (175°C).
2. Spread the hazelnuts evenly on a baking sheet and roast them in the oven for about 12-15 minutes or until the skins crack.
3. Remove the hazelnuts from the oven and place them on a clean kitchen towel. Fold the towel over the hazelnuts and rub them together to remove as much skin as possible.
4. Transfer the skinless hazelnuts to a food processor or high-speed blender.
5. Add the cocoa powder, powdered sugar or sweetener, vanilla extract, and salt (if using).
6. Blend the mixture on medium-high speed, occasionally scraping down the sides of the container. The hazelnuts

will eventually turn into a smooth, chocolatey hazelnut spread.
7. Taste and adjust sweetness according to your preference.
8. Transfer the chocolate-hazelnut indulgence to a clean,

CREAMY COCONUT MACADAMIA BUTTER:

INGREDIENTS:

- 1 1/2 cups of raw macadamia nuts
- 1/2 cup of unsweetened shredded coconut
- One tbsp of coconut oil
- 1/4 tsp salt (optional)

INSTRUCTIONS:

1. Preheat your oven to 350°F (175°C).
2. Spread the macadamia nuts and shredded coconut on a baking sheet and roast them in the oven for about 8-10 minutes or until lightly toasted.
3. Let the macadamia nuts and coconut cool for a few minutes.
4. Transfer the roasted macadamia nuts and coconut to a food processor or high-speed blender.
5. Add the coconut oil and salt (if using).
6. Blend the mixture on medium-high speed, occasionally scraping down the sides of the container. The macadamia nuts and coconut will gradually transform into creamy coconut macadamia butter.
7. Taste and adjust saltiness according to your preference.
8. Transfer the creamy coconut macadamia butter for a few weeks.

HONEY-ROASTED PEANUT BUTTER:

INGREDIENTS:

- 2 cups of roasted peanuts
- Two tbsp honey
- One tbsp of vegetable oil
- 1/2 tsp salt (optional)

INSTRUCTIONS:

1. In a food processor or high-powered blender, add the roasted peanuts.
2. Blend the peanuts quickly until they become a smooth and creamy butter consistency. This may take a few minutes, and you may need to occasionally stop and scrape down the sides of the processor/blender
3. Add honey and vegetable oil once the peanuts have reached the desired creamy texture. Blend again until everything is well combined.
4. Taste the peanut butter and add salt if desired for a salted version. Blend once more to incorporate the salt.
5. Transfer the honey-roasted peanut butter to a jar or airtight container. Store it in the refrigerator for up to a few weeks.

SPICY CACAO BRAZIL NUT BUTTER:

INGREDIENTS:

- 2 cups of Brazil nuts
- Two tbsp cacao powder (unsweetened)
- One tbsp of maple syrup or agave syrup
- 1/2 tsp ground cinnamon
- 1/4 tsp cayenne pepper (adjust to your desired level of spiciness)
- Pinch of salt

INSTRUCTIONS:

1. In a food processor or high-powered blender, add the Brazil nuts.
2. Blend the Brazil nuts on high speed until they form a creamy butter consistency, similar to peanut butter.
3. Add the cacao powder, maple syrup or agave syrup, ground cinnamon, cayenne pepper, and a pinch of salt to the Brazil nut butter.
4. Blend again until all the ingredients are well combined and the nut butter has a smooth texture.
5. Taste and adjust the sweetness or spiciness according to your preference.
6. Transfer the spicy cacao Brazil nut butter to a jar or airtight container. Store it in the refrigerator for up to a few weeks.

VANILLA-WALNUT BUTTER DELIGHT:

INGREDIENTS:

- 2 cups of walnuts
- Two tbsp of maple syrup
- One tsp of vanilla extract
- Pinch of salt

INSTRUCTIONS:

1. In a food processor or high-powered blender, add the walnuts.
2. Blend the walnuts quickly until they become a smooth and creamy butter consistency.
3. Add the maple syrup, vanilla extract, and a pinch of salt to the walnut butter.
4. Blend again until all the ingredients are well combined and the nut butter has a smooth texture.
5. Taste and adjust the sweetness or saltiness according to your preference.
6. Transfer the vanilla-walnut butter delight to a jar or airtight container. Store it in the refrigerator for up to a few weeks.

SALTED PISTACHIO BUTTER INFUSION:

INGREDIENTS:

- 2 cups of shelled pistachios (roasted or raw)
- One tbsp of honey or agave syrup
- 1/2 tsp sea salt (adjust to taste)
- One tbsp of vegetable oil (optional for a creamier texture)

INSTRUCTIONS:

1. In a food processor or high-powered blender, add the pistachios.
2. Blend the pistachios quickly until they form a smooth and creamy butter consistency.
3. Add the honey, agave syrup, and sea salt to the pistachio butter.
4. Optionally, add a tbsp of vegetable oil to achieve a creamier texture.

5. Blend again until all the ingredients are well combined.
6. Taste and adjust the sweetness or saltiness according to your preference.
7. Transfer the salted pistachio butter infusion to a jar or airtight container. Store it in the refrigerator for up to a few weeks.

ESPRESSO-SESAME SEED BUTTER:

INGREDIENTS:

- 1 1/2 cups of roasted sesame seeds
- One tbsp of espresso powder or finely ground coffee
- Two tbsp of maple syrup
- 1/2 tsp vanilla extract
- Pinch of salt

INSTRUCTIONS:

1. In a food processor or high-powered blender, add the roasted sesame seeds.
2. Blend the sesame seeds on high speed until they start to release their oils and form a paste.
3. Add the espresso powder or finely ground coffee, maple syrup, vanilla extract, and a pinch of salt to the sesame seed paste.
4. Blend again until all the ingredients are well combined and the nut butter has a smooth texture.
5. Taste and adjust the sweetness or saltiness according to your preference.
6. Transfer the espresso-sesame seed butter to a jar or airtight container. Store it in the refrigerator for up to a few weeks.

HEALTHY SNACKS AND DIPS:

CREAMY AVOCADO HUMMUS:

INGREDIENTS:

- One ripe avocado
- One can (15 Ounces) chickpeas, drained and rinsed
- Two cloves garlic, minced
- Three tbsp tahini
- Three tbsp fresh lemon juice
- Two tbsp of olive oil
- 1/2 tsp ground cumin
- Salt and pepper to taste
- Water (as needed for consistency)

INSTRUCTIONS:

1. Combine the avocado, chickpeas, garlic, tahini, lemon juice, olive oil, cumin, salt, and pepper in a food processor.
2. Process the mixture until smooth and creamy. If the hummus is too thick, add water gradually until you reach your desired consistency.
3. Taste and adjust seasoning if needed.
4. Transfer the hummus to a serving bowl and garnish with olive oil, paprika, and fresh parsley.
5. Serve with pita bread, tortilla chips, or vegetable sticks for dipping.

GREEK YOGURT SPINACH DIP:

INGREDIENTS:

- 1 cup of Greek yogurt
- 1 cup of chopped spinach (frOuncesen and thawed or freshly cooked and squeezed dry)
- 1/4 cup of grated Parmesan cheese
- 1/4 cup of mayonnaise
- Two cloves garlic, minced
- One tbsp of lemon juice
- 1/2 tsp onion powder
- Salt and pepper to taste

INSTRUCTIONS:

1. Combine the Greek yogurt, chopped spinach, Parmesan cheese, mayonnaise, minced garlic, lemon juice, and onion powder in a mixing bowl.
2. Mix well until all the ingredients are thoroughly combined.
3. Season with salt and pepper to taste.
4. Cover the bowl and refrigerate the dip for at least 1 hour before serving to allow the flavors to meld.
5. Serve the dip with pita chips, crackers, or vegetable sticks.

ROASTED RED PEPPER AND WALNUT DIP:

INGREDIENTS:

- Two large red bell peppers
- 1/2 cup of walnuts
- 1/4 cup of breadcrumbs
- Two cloves garlic, minced
- Two tbsp of olive oil
- One tbsp of lemon juice
- One tsp of ground cumin

- Salt and pepper to taste
- Fresh parsley for garnish

INSTRUCTIONS:

1. Preheat your oven to 400°F (200°C).
2. Cut the red bell peppers in half, remove the seeds and stems, place them on a baking sheet, and cut side down.
3. Roast the peppers in the oven for about 20-25 minutes or until the skins are blistered and blackened.
4. Remove the peppers from the oven and let them cool. Once cool, peel off the blackened skins.
5. Combine the roasted red peppers, walnuts, breadcrumbs, minced garlic, olive oil, lemon juice, ground cumin, salt, and pepper in a food processor.
6. Process the mixture until smooth and creamy.
7. Transfer the dip to a serving bowl, garnish with fresh parsley, and drizzle with olive oil.
8. Serve the dip with pita bread, breadsticks, or vegetable crudités.

ZUCCHINI FRIES WITH LEMON-DILL DIP:

INGREDIENTS

- Two large zucchinis, cut into thin strips
- 1 cup of all-purpose flour
- Two eggs, beaten
- 1 cup of breadcrumbs
- 1/2 cup of grated Parmesan cheese
- One tsp paprika
- Salt and pepper to taste
- Cooking spray or oil for greasing
- Ingredients for Lemon-Dill Dip:

- 1 cup of Greek yogurt
- One tbsp of fresh dill, chopped
- One tbsp of lemon juice
- One tsp of lemon zest
- One clove of garlic, minced
- Salt and pepper to taste

INSTRUCTIONS

1. Preheat your oven to 425°F (220°C) and grease a baking sheet with cooking spray or oil.
2. Place the flour, beaten eggs, and breadcrumbs mixed with grated Parmesan, paprika, salt, and pepper in separate bowls.
3. Dip each zucchini strip into the flour, then the beaten eggs, and finally, coat with the breadcrumb mixture. Press the breadcrumbs onto the zucchini to adhere well.
4. Place the coated zucchini strips in a single layer on the prepared baking sheet.
5. Bake in the oven for about 20-25 minutes or until the zucchini fries are golden and crispy.

SPICY CHICKPEA SNACK MIX:

INGREDIENTS:

- 2 cups of cooked chickpeas (canned or cooked from dry)
- One tbsp of olive oil
- One tsp of ground cumin
- 1/2 tsp chili powder
- 1/2 tsp paprika
- 1/4 tsp cayenne pepper (adjust to your spice preference)
- 1/2 tsp garlic powder
- 1/2 tsp onion powder

- Salt to taste

INSTRUCTIONS:

1. Preheat your oven to 400°F (200°C) and line a baking sheet with parchment paper.
2. Toss the cooked chickpeas with olive oil in a mixing bowl until well coated.
3. Mix the ground cumin, chili powder, paprika, cayenne pepper, garlic powder, onion powder, and salt in a separate small bowl.
4. Sprinkle the spice mixture over the chickpeas and toss until evenly coated.
5. Spread the seasoned chickpeas in a single layer on the prepared baking sheet.
6. Bake in the preheated oven for about 20-25 minutes or until the chickpeas are crispy and golden, stirring them once or twice during baking to ensure even cooking.

CUCUMBER SLICES WITH TZATZIKI SAUCE:

INGREDIENTS:

- Two large cucumbers
- 1 cup of Greek yogurt
- 1/4 cup of grated cucumber
- Two cloves garlic, minced
- One tbsp of fresh lemon juice
- One tbsp of fresh dill, chopped
- One tbsp of fresh mint, chopped
- Salt and pepper to taste

INSTRUCTIONS:

1. Wash the cucumbers and slice them into thin rounds.

2. Combine Greek yogurt, grated cucumber, minced garlic, lemon juice, dill, mint, salt, and pepper in a mixing bowl. Mix well.
3. Taste and adjust seasoning as needed.
4. Serve the cucumber slices with the tzatziki sauce on the side. You can garnish with extra dill and mint if desired.

SWEET POTATO CHIPS WITH GUACAMOLE:

INGREDIENTS:

- Two large sweet potatoes
- Two tbsp of olive oil
- 1 tsp paprika
- One tsp of garlic powder
- Salt and pepper to taste
- For the Guacamole:
- Three ripe avocados
- One small red onion, finely chopped
- 1-2 tomatoes, diced
- One jalapeno, seeds removed and finely chopped (optional)
- One lime, juiced
- Two tbsp fresh cilantro chopped
- Salt and pepper to taste

INSTRUCTIONS:

1. Preheat the oven to 400°F (200°C).
2. Wash and peel the sweet potatoes. Slice them thinly using a mandoline slicer or a sharp knife.
3. Toss the sweet potato slices in a large bowl with olive oil, paprika, garlic powder, salt, and pepper until evenly coated.

4. Arrange the sweet potato slices on a baking sheet lined with parchment paper, ensuring they don't overlap.
5. Bake for 15-20 minutes or until the sweet potato chips are crispy and golden brown. Flip them halfway through the baking time for even cooking.
6. While the sweet potato chips are baking, prepare the guacamole. In a bowl, mash the avocados with a fork until smooth but still slightly chunky.
7. Add the chopped red onion, diced tomatoes, jalapeno (if using), lime juice, cilantro, salt, and pepper to the mashed avocados. Mix well.
8. Taste and adjust seasoning as needed.
9. Once the sweet potato chips are ready, serve them with the guacamole on the side.

BUFFALO CAULIFLOWER BITES:

INGREDIENTS:

- One large head of cauliflower, cut into bite-sized florets
- 1 cup of all-purpose flour (or gluten-free flour for a GF version)
- 1 cup of milk (or plant-based milk for a vegan version)
- One tsp of garlic powder
- One tsp of onion powder
- 1/2 tsp paprika
- Salt and pepper to taste
- 1 cup of buffalo sauce (store-bought or homemade)
- Two tbsp melted butter (or vegan butter for a vegan version)

INSTRUCTIONS:

1. Preheat the oven to 450°F (230°C). Line a baking sheet with parchment paper or lightly grease it.
2. Whisk together the flour, milk, garlic powder, onion powder, paprika, salt, and pepper in a large bowl to create a smooth batter.
3. Dip each cauliflower floret into the batter, making sure it's coated evenly, and place it on the prepared baking sheet.
4. Bake the cauliflower for about 20-25 minutes or until golden and crispy.
5. In a separate bowl, mix the buffalo sauce and melted butter.
6. Once the cauliflower bites are done baking, toss them in the buffalo sauce mixture until they are fully coated.
7. Serve immediately with your choice of dipping sauce on the side.

CARROT AND BEETROOT DIP:

INGREDIENTS:

- Two large carrots, peeled and chopped
- One medium beetroot, peeled and chopped
- 1/4 cup of Greek yogurt (or sour cream for a creamier dip)
- Two tbsp tahini
- Two tbsp of lemon juice
- One clove of garlic, minced
- Two tbsp of olive oil
- Salt and pepper to taste
- Water (if needed for consistency)

INSTRUCTIONS:

1. Steam or boil the chopped carrots and beetroot until they are tender.
2. Add the cooked carrots, beetroot, Greek yogurt, tahini, lemon juice, minced garlic, olive oil, salt, and pepper in a food processor.
3. Blend until smooth. If the dip is too thick, add water to reach your desired consistency.
4. Taste and adjust seasoning as needed.
5. Transfer the dip to a serving bowl and drizzle olive oil on top for garnish.

EDAMAME AND MINT HUMMUS:

INGREDIENTS:

- 1 cup of shelled edamame (cooked according to package instructions)
- 1/4 cup of fresh mint leaves
- 1/4 cup of tahini
- Two tbsp of lemon juice
- One clove of garlic, minced
- Two tbsp of olive oil
- Salt and pepper to taste
- Water (if needed for consistency)

INSTRUCTIONS:

1. Combine the cooked edamame, fresh mint leaves, tahini, lemon juice, minced garlic, olive oil, salt, and pepper in a food processor.
2. Blend until smooth. Add a little water to achieve your desired consistency if the hummus is too thick.
3. Taste and adjust seasoning as needed.

4. Transfer the hummus to a serving bowl and drizzle with olive oil and some extra mint leaves for garnish.

DETOX AND CLEANSING BLENDS:

GREEN DETOXIFYING ELIXIR:

INGREDIENTS:

- 2 cups of fresh spinach leaves
- One medium cucumber peeled and chopped
- One green apple, cored and chopped
- 1/2 lemon, juiced
- 1-inch piece of fresh ginger peeled
- 1 cup of water or coconut water

INSTRUCTIONS:

1. Wash the spinach leaves thoroughly.
2. In a blender, add all the ingredients and blend until smooth.
3. Add more or coconut water to reach your desired consistency if the consistency is too thick.
4. Pour into a glass and enjoy immediately.

LEMON GINGER CLEANSER:

INGREDIENTS:

- One lemon, juiced
- 1-inch piece of fresh ginger, grated or finely chopped
- One tbsp honey
- 2 cups of water

INSTRUCTIONS:

1. Mix the lemon juice, grated ginger, and honey in a glass.
2. Heat the water until it's warm (not boiling), and then pour it into the glass with the lemon-ginger mixture.
3. Stir well until the honey is dissolved.
4. Let it steep for a few minutes to infuse the flavors.
5. Strain the mixture to remove any ginger pieces if desired.
6. Sip slowly and enjoy the cleansing benefits.

DETOXIFYING BEET BLAST:

INGREDIENTS:

- One medium beetroot, peeled and chopped
- One carrot, peeled and chopped
- One orange, peeled and segmented
- 1 cup of water or coconut water
- Optional: 1 tbsp chia seeds

INSTRUCTIONS:

1. Wash and prepare the beetroot, carrot, and orange.
2. In a blender, add all the ingredients and blend until smooth.
3. If you prefer a thicker texture or added nutrition, you can include chia seeds and let the mixture sit for a few minutes to allow the roots to expand.
4. Pour the detoxifying beet blast into a glass and serve chilled.

CLEANSING CUCUMBER-MINT COOLER:

INGREDIENTS:

- Two medium cucumbers peeled and chopped
- 1/4 cup of fresh mint leaves

- One lime, juiced
- 2 cups of water or coconut water
- Ice cubes

INSTRUCTIONS:

1. Add chopped cucumbers, fresh mint leaves, and lime juice in a blender.
2. Blend until smooth.
3. Add water or coconut water and blend again until well combined.
4. Fill a glass with ice cubes and pour the cucumber-mint cooler over the ice.
5. Stir gently and enjoy the refreshing cleanse.

BLUEBERRY-CABBAGE DETOX BLEND:

INGREDIENTS:

- 1 cup of blueberries (fresh or frOuncesen)
- 1 cup of shredded purple cabbage
- One tbsp of lemon juice
- One tbsp of honey or maple syrup
- 1 1/2 cups of water or almond milk

INSTRUCTIONS:

1. Wash the blueberries and cabbage.
2. Add the blueberries, shredded cabbage, lemon juice, honey (or maple syrup), and water or almond milk in a blender.
3. Blend until you get a smooth and creamy texture.
4. Pour the detox blend into a glass and savor the unique flavors.

PINEAPPLE-MATCHA DETOX SMOOTHIE:

INGREDIENTS:

- 1 cup of chopped pineapple
- One tsp of matcha powder
- 1/2 cucumber, peeled and chopped
- 1 cup of spinach leaves
- One tbsp of chia seeds
- 1 cup of coconut water
- 1/2 cup of ice cubes (optional)

INSTRUCTIONS:

1. Combine chopped pineapple, matcha powder, cucumber, spinach, chia seeds, and coconut water in a blender.
2. Blend on high speed until the mixture is smooth and creamy.
3. If you prefer a colder smoothie, add ice cubes and blend again.
4. Pour the smoothie into a glass and enjoy your Pineapple-Matcha Detox Smoothie.

GINGER-LEMON APPLE CLEANSE:

INGREDIENTS:

- Two apples, cored and chopped
- 1-inch piece of fresh ginger, peeled and grated
- Juice of 1 lemon
- 1 cup of water
- 1 tbsp honey (optional)

INSTRUCTIONS:

1. Place the chopped apples, grated ginger, lemon juice, and water in a blender.
2. Blend until you get a smooth mixture.
3. Taste the mixture and add honey if you prefer a sweeter taste.
4. Pour the Ginger-Lemon Apple Cleanse into a glass and serve immediately.

CRANBERRY DETOX REFRESHER:

INGREDIENTS:

- 1 cup of fresh or frOuncesen cranberries
- 1/2 cup of cucumber, chopped
- One small orange, peeled and segmented
- One tbsp of fresh mint leaves
- 1 cup of coconut water
- 1/2 cup of ice cubes (optional)

INSTRUCTIONS:

1. Combine cranberries, chopped cucumber, orange segments, mint leaves, and coconut water in a blender.
2. Blend until you achieve a smooth consistency.
3. If you want a chilled drink, add ice cubes and blend again.
4. Pour the Cranberry Detox Refresher into a glass and enjoy.

TURMERIC DETOX POWERHOUSE:

INGREDIENTS:

- One ripe banana
- 1/2 cup of pineapple chunks
- One tsp of turmeric powder (or use fresh turmeric root)

- 1/2 tsp ground cinnamon
- One tbsp of freshly grated ginger
- 1 cup of almond milk (or any plant-based milk)
- 1/2 cup of plain Greek yogurt (or coconut yogurt for a vegan option)

INSTRUCTIONS:

1. Combine the ripe banana, pineapple chunks, turmeric powder, ground cinnamon, freshly grated ginger, almond milk, and Greek yogurt in a blender.
2. Blend until smooth and creamy.
3. You can add more yogurt or a few ice cubes if you want a thicker consistency.
4. Pour the Turmeric Detox Powerhouse smoothie into a glass and enjoy.

PAPAYA-PARSLEY CLEANSING BLEND:

INGREDIENTS:

- 1 cup of ripe papaya, peeled and deseeded
- 1/2 cup of fresh parsley leaves
- Juice of 1 lime
- One tbsp flaxseeds
- 1 cup of coconut water
- 1/2 cup of ice cubes (optional)

INSTRUCTIONS:

1. Combine ripe papaya, fresh parsley leaves, lime juice, flaxseeds, and coconut water in a blender.
2. Blend until smooth and well-mixed.
3. For a colder drink, add ice cubes and blend again.

4. Pour the Papaya-Parsley Cleansing Blend into a glass and serve.

INDULGENT DESSERT SMOOTHIES:

CHOCOLATE BANANA DREAM SHAKE:

INGREDIENTS:

- Two ripe bananas
- 1 cup of milk (dairy or plant-based)
- Two tbsp of cocoa powder
- One tbsp of honey or maple syrup
- 1/2 tsp vanilla extract
- 1 cup of ice cubes

INSTRUCTIONS:

1. Peel the bananas and place them in a blender.
2. Add the milk, cocoa powder, honey (or maple syrup), and vanilla extract to the blender.
3. Blend all the ingredients until smooth.
4. Add the ice cubes and blend until the mixture becomes creamy and frothy.
5. Pour the shake into glasses and enjoy your Chocolate Banana Dream Shake!

VANILLA ALMOND DATE SMOOTHIE:

INGREDIENTS:

- 1 cup of almond milk
- 1/2 cup of plain Greek yogurt

- Two tbsp of almond butter
- 4 Medjool dates, pitted
- One tsp of vanilla extract
- 1 cup of ice cubes

INSTRUCTIONS:

1. Combine the almond milk, Greek yogurt, almond butter, pitted dates, and vanilla extract in a blender.
2. Blend the ingredients until the mixture is smooth and the dates are fully incorporated.
3. Add the ice cubes to the blender and blend until the smoothie is thick and creamy.
4. Pour the Vanilla Almond Date Smoothie into glasses and savor the delightful flavor!

STRAWBERRY CHEESECAKE DELIGHT:

INGREDIENTS:

- 1 cup of frOuncesen strawberries
- 1/2 cup of cream cheese
- 1 cup of milk (dairy or plant-based)
- Two tbsp of honey or agave syrup
- One tsp of lemon juice
- 1/2 tsp vanilla extract
- 1 cup of ice cubes

INSTRUCTIONS:

1. Place the frOuncesen strawberries, cream cheese, milk, honey (or agave syrup), lemon juice, and vanilla extract in a blender.
2. Blend all the ingredients until the mixture is creamy and smooth.

3. Add the ice cubes to the blender and blend until the smoothie is thick.
4. Pour the Strawberry Cheesecake Delight into glasses and enjoy the delicious taste!

MINT CHOCOLATE CHIP INDULGENCE:

INGREDIENTS:

- 2 cups of milk (dairy or plant-based)
- 1 cup of fresh spinach leaves
- 1/2 tsp peppermint extract
- One tbsp of honey or maple syrup
- 1/4 cup of dark chocolate chips
- 1 cup of ice cubes

INSTRUCTIONS:

1. Pour the milk into a blender and add the fresh spinach leaves, peppermint extract, honey (or maple syrup), and dark chocolate chips.
2. Blend the ingredients until the mixture is smooth and the spinach is thoroughly blended.
3. Add the ice cubes to the blender and blend until the smoothie is thick and creamy.
4. Pour the Mint Chocolate Chip Indulgence into glasses and relish the refreshing and indulgent taste!

PEANUT BUTTER CUP OF SMOOTHIE:

INGREDIENTS:

- Two ripe bananas
- Two tbsp of peanut butter
- 1 cup of milk (dairy or plant-based)

- One tbsp of cocoa powder
- 1 tbsp honey or agave syrup
- 1/2 tsp vanilla extract
- 1 cup of ice cubes

INSTRUCTIONS:

1. Peel the bananas and place them in a blender.
2. Add the peanut butter, milk, cocoa powder, honey (or agave syrup), and vanilla extract to the blender.
3. Blend all the ingredients until the mixture is creamy and smooth.
4. Add the ice cubes to the blender and blend again until the smoothie is thick and well combined.
5. Pour the Peanut Butter Cup of Smoothie into glasses and enjoy the delightful combination of flavors!

RASPBERRY WHITE CHOCOLATE BLISS

INGREDIENTS:

- 1 cup of fresh or fr0uncesen raspberries
- 1/2 cup of white chocolate chips
- 1 cup of vanilla ice cream
- 1/2 cup of milk
- Whipped cream (for topping, optional)
- Fresh raspberries (for garnish, optional)

INSTRUCTIONS:

1. Combine the raspberries, white chocolate chips, vanilla ice cream, and milk in a blender.
2. Blend until the mixture is smooth and creamy.
3. If desired, pour the smoothie into a glass and top with whipped cream and fresh raspberries.

4. Serve immediately and enjoy!

BLACK FOREST CHERRY SMOOTHIE

INGREDIENTS:

- 1 cup of fr0uncesen cherries
- 1/2 cup of chocolate chips
- 1 cup of plain or vanilla yogurt
- 1/2 cup of milk
- Chocolate shavings (for topping, optional)
- Maraschino cherries (for garnish, optional)

INSTRUCTIONS:

1. Combine the fr0uncesen cherries, chocolate chips, yogurt, and milk in a blender.
2. Blend until the mixture is smooth and well combined.
3. If desired, pour the smoothie into a glass and top with chocolate shavings and a maraschino cherry.
4. Serve immediately and enjoy!

COCONUT MANGO SORBET SHAKE

INGREDIENTS:

- 1 cup of mango chunks (fresh or fr0uncesen)
- 1/2 cup of coconut milk
- 1/2 cup of vanilla ice cream or mango sorbet
- 1/4 cup of shredded coconut
- Toasted coconut flakes (for topping, optional)
- Mango slices (for garnish, optional)

INSTRUCTIONS:

1. Combine the mango chunks, coconut milk, vanilla ice cream, mango sorbet, and shredded coconut in a blender.
2. Blend until the mixture is smooth and creamy.
3. If desired, pour the shake into a glass and top with toasted coconut flakes and mango slices.
4. Serve immediately and enjoy!

COOKIES AND CREAM FANTASY

INGREDIENTS:

- 1 cup of vanilla ice cream
- 1/2 cup of crushed chocolate cookies (like Oreos)
- 1/4 cup of milk
- Chocolate sauce (for topping, optional)
- Crushed cookies (for garnish, optional)

INSTRUCTIONS:

1. Combine the vanilla ice cream, crushed chocolate cookies, and milk in a blender.
2. Blend until the mixture is smooth and the cookies are fully incorporated.
3. If desired, pour the shake into a glass and drizzle chocolate sauce on top.
4. Sprinkle some crushed cookies as a garnish, if desired.
5. Serve immediately and enjoy!

SALTED CARAMEL PRETZEL DELIGHT

INGREDIENTS:

- 1 cup of caramel ice cream
- 1/2 cup of pretzels
- 1/4 cup of milk

- Whipped cream (for topping, optional)
- Caramel sauce (for topping, optional)
- Pretzel sticks (for garnish, optional)

INSTRUCTIONS:

1. Combine the caramel ice cream, pretzels, and milk in a blender.
2. Blend until the mixture is smooth and the pretzels are crushed and mixed in.
3. If desired, pour the shake into a glass and top with whipped cream and a drizzle of caramel sauce.
4. Add a pretzel stick as a garnish, if desired.
5. Serve immediately and enjoy!

HYDRATING SUMMER SIPS:

WATERMELON-LIME COOLER:

INGREDIENTS:

- 4 cups of diced watermelon (seeds removed)
- Juice of 2 limes
- 1/4 cup of fresh mint leaves
- 2 cups of cold water
- Ice cubes
- Lime slices and mint sprigs for garnish (optional)

INSTRUCTIONS:

1. Combine the diced watermelon, lime juice, and fresh mint leaves in a blender.
2. Blend until smooth and well combined.

3. Pour the mixture through a fine-mesh strainer into a pitcher to remove any pulp.
4. Add cold water to the pitcher and stir well.
5. Fill glasses with ice cubes and pour the watermelon-lime mixture over the ice.
6. Garnish with lime slices and mint sprigs, if desired.
7. Serve immediately and enjoy!

PINEAPPLE MINT REFRESHER:

INGREDIENTS:

- 2 cups of fresh pineapple chunks
- 1/4 cup of fresh mint leaves
- One tbsp of honey or agave syrup (optional, adjust to taste)
- 2 cups of sparkling water
- Ice cubes
- Pineapple wedges and mint sprigs for garnish (optional)

INSTRUCTIONS:

1. In a blender, combine the fresh pineapple chunks, mint leaves, and honey or agave syrup (if using).
2. Blend until smooth and well combined.
3. Pour the mixture through a fine-mesh strainer into a pitcher to remove any fiber.
4. Add sparkling water to the pitcher and stir gently.
5. Fill glasses with ice cubes and pour the pineapple mint mixture over the ice.
6. Garnish with pineapple wedges and mint sprigs, if desired.
7. Serve immediately and enjoy!

CUCUMBER-LEMONADE SPLASH:

INGREDIENTS:

- 2 cups of fresh cucumber slices (peeled and seeds removed)
- Juice of 4 lemons
- 1/4 cup of fresh basil leaves
- 1/4 cup of granulated sugar or honey (adjust to taste)
- 2 cups of cold water
- Ice cubes
- Lemon slices and basil sprigs for garnish (optional)

INSTRUCTIONS:

1. Combine the fresh cucumber slices, lemon juice, basil leaves, and sugar or honey in a blender.
2. Blend until smooth and well combined.
3. Pour the mixture through a fine-mesh strainer into a pitcher to remove any seeds or large pieces.
4. Add cold water to the pitcher and stir well.
5. Fill glasses with ice cubes and pour the cucumber-lemonade mixture over the ice.
6. Garnish with lemon slices and basil sprigs, if desired.
7. Serve immediately and enjoy!

HONEYDEW-BASIL BREEZE:

INGREDIENTS:

- 4 cups of diced honeydew melon (seeds removed)
- 1/4 cup of fresh basil leaves
- Juice of 1 lime
- 2 cups of coconut water (or regular water if preferred)
- Ice cubes

- Honeydew balls and basil sprigs for garnish (optional)

INSTRUCTIONS:

1. Combine the diced honeydew melon, fresh basil leaves, and lime juice in a blender.
2. Blend until smooth and well combined.
3. Pour the mixture through a fine-mesh strainer into a pitcher to remove any pulp.
4. Add coconut water to the pitcher and stir well.
5. Fill glasses with ice cubes and pour the honeydew-basil mixture over the ice.
6. Garnish with honeydew balls and basil sprigs, if desired.
7. Serve immediately and enjoy!

MANGO-PEACH ICED TEA:

INGREDIENTS:

- Two ripe mangoes, peeled and diced
- Two ripe peaches, peeled and diced
- 4 cups of brewed black tea (cooled to room temperature)
- Two tbsp honey or maple syrup (adjust to taste)
- Ice cubes
- Mango and peach slices for garnish (optional)

INSTRUCTIONS:

1. Combine the diced mangoes, diced peaches, and honey or maple syrup in a blender.
2. Blend until smooth and well combined.
3. Pour the mixture through a fine-mesh strainer into a pitcher to remove fiber or pulp.
4. Add brewed black tea to the pitcher and stir well.

5. Fill glasses with ice cubes and pour the mango-peach iced tea over the ice.
6. Garnish with mango and peach slices, if desired.
7. Serve immediately and enjoy!

RASPBERRY-LEMON SPARKLER:

INGREDIENTS:

- 1 cup of fresh raspberries
- 1/2 cup of freshly squeezed lemon juice
- Two tbsp honey or agave syrup (adjust to taste)
- 2 cups of sparkling water or Club soda
- Ice cubes
- Lemon slices and fresh raspberries for garnish

INSTRUCTIONS:

1. In a blender, puree the fresh raspberries until smooth.
2. Combine the raspberry puree, freshly squeezed lemon juice, and honey/agave syrup in a pitcher.
3. Stir well until the sweetener is fully dissolved.
4. Add ice cubes to the pitcher and pour the sparkling water or club soda.
5. Stir gently to combine all the ingredients.
6. Pour into glasses, garnish with lemon slices and fresh raspberries, and serve immediately.

BLUEBERRY-LAVENDER LEMONADE:

INGREDIENTS:

- 1 cup of fresh blueberries
- One tbsp of dried lavender buds or 2-3 fresh lavender sprigs

- 1/2 cup of freshly squeezed lemon juice
- 1/4 cup of honey or maple syrup (adjust to taste)
- 4 cups of water
- Ice cubes
- Fresh lavender sprigs and blueberries for garnish

INSTRUCTIONS:

1. Combine the fresh blueberries, lavender buds or sprigs, and 1 cup of water in a small saucepan.
2. Bring the mixture to a simmer over low heat and let it simmer for 5 minutes.
3. Remove the saucepan from the heat and allow the blueberry-lavender mixture to cool.
4. Strain the mixture to remove the solids, pressing down on the blueberries and lavender to extract the flavors.
5. Combine the freshly squeezed lemon juice, honey/maple syrup, and the remaining 3 cups of water in a pitcher.
6. Add the strained blueberry-lavender mixture to the pitcher and stir well to combine.
7. Add ice cubes to the pitcher and stir again.
8. Pour into glasses, garnish with fresh lavender sprigs and blueberries, and serve chilled.

KIWI-COCONUT WATER QUENCHER:

INGREDIENTS:

- Two ripe kiwis, peeled and sliced
- 4 cups of coconut water
- One tbsp of lime juice
- One tbsp of honey or agave syrup (adjust to taste)
- Ice cubes
- Kiwi slices and mint leaves for garnish

INSTRUCTIONS:

1. In a blender, puree the ripe kiwis until smooth.
2. Combine the kiwi puree, coconut water, lime juice, and honey/agave syrup in a pitcher.
3. Stir well until the sweetener is fully dissolved.
4. Add ice cubes to the pitcher and stir again.
5. Pour into glasses, garnish with kiwi slices and mint leaves, and serve chilled.

STRAWBERRY-BASIL INFUSED WATER:

INGREDIENTS:

- 1 cup of fresh strawberries, hulled and sliced
- 8-10 fresh basil leaves
- 4 cups of water
- Ice cubes

INSTRUCTIONS:

1. In a large pitcher, combine the fresh strawberry slices and basil leaves.
2. Pour in the water and stir gently.
3. Cover the pitcher and refrigerate for at least 1 hour (or overnight) to allow the flavors to infuse.
4. Before serving, add ice cubes to the pitcher.
5. Pour into glasses, and add some infused strawberry and basil pieces to each glass for extra flavor and presentation.

CITRUSY HIBISCUS PUNCH:

INGREDIENTS:

- 2 cups of hibiscus tea (prepared by steeping two tbsp of dried hibiscus flowers in 4 cups of hot water and letting it cool)
- 1 cup of freshly squeezed orange juice
- 1/2 cup of freshly squeezed lemon juice
- Two tbsp honey or agave syrup (adjust to taste)
- 1 cup of sparkling water or Club soda
- Orange and lemon slices for garnish
- Ice cubes

INSTRUCTIONS:

1. Combine the hibiscus tea, freshly squeezed orange juice, freshly squeezed lemon juice, and honey/agave syrup in a pitcher.
2. Stir well until the sweetener is fully dissolved.
3. Add ice cubes to the pitcher and pour the sparkling water or club soda.
4. Stir gently to combine all the ingredients.
5. Pour into glasses, garnish with orange and lemon slices, and serve chilled.

NUTRIBULLET MOCKTAILS: NON-ALCOHOLIC BLENDS:

VIRGIN PIÑA COLADA:

INGREDIENTS:

- 1 cup of pineapple juice
- 1/2 cup of coconut cream

- 1/2 cup of crushed ice
- Pineapple wedge and maraschino cherry for garnish

INSTRUCTIONS:

1. Combine the pineapple juice, coconut cream, and crushed ice in a blender.
2. Blend until smooth and creamy.
3. Pour the mixture into a tall glass.
4. Garnish with a pineapple wedge and a maraschino cherry on top.
5. Serve immediately and enjoy your refreshing Virgin Piña Colada!

STRAWBERRY MOJITO MOCKTAIL:

INGREDIENTS:

- 1 cup of fresh strawberries, hulled and halved
- Ten fresh mint leaves
- 1/2 lime, juiced
- Two tbsp simple syrup (or adjust to taste)
- 1 cup of sparkling water
- Crushed ice
- Strawberry slices and mint sprigs for garnish

INSTRUCTIONS:

1. Muddle the strawberries and mint leaves together in a cocktail shaker or a tall glass.
2. Add the lime juice and simple syrup to the shaker/glass and gently stir.
3. Fill the glass with crushed ice.
4. Top it off with sparkling water.
5. Garnish with strawberry slices and mint sprigs.

6. Stir gently, and your Strawberry Mojito Mocktail is ready to be served.

BLUEBERRY BASIL SMASH:

INGREDIENTS:

- 1/2 cup of fresh blueberries
- 4-5 fresh basil leaves
- 1/2 lemon, juiced
- Two tbsp of honey or simple syrup
- 1 cup of soda water or sparkling water
- Ice cubes
- Fresh blueberries and basil leaves for garnish

INSTRUCTIONS:

1. Muddle the fresh blueberries and basil leaves together in a cocktail shaker or a tall glass.
2. Add the lemon juice and honey (or simple syrup) to the shaker/glass and stir well.
3. Fill the glass with ice cubes.
4. Top it off with soda water or sparkling water.
5. Could you give it a gentle stir?
6. Garnish with fresh blueberries and a few basil leaves on top.
7. Enjoy your delightful Blueberry Basil Smash mocktail!

CUCUMBER COOLER MOCKTAIL:

INGREDIENTS:

- 1 cup of cucumber, peeled and sliced
- 1/2 lime, juiced
- One tbsp of agave syrup or honey

- 1 cup of tonic water or club soda
- Ice cubes
- Cucumber slices and mint sprigs for garnish

INSTRUCTIONS:

1. In a cocktail shaker or a tall glass, muddle the cucumber slices.
2. Add the lime juice and agave syrup (or honey) to the shaker/glass and stir well.
3. Fill the glass with ice cubes.
4. Top it off with tonic water or club soda.
5. Could you give it a gentle stir?
6. Garnish with cucumber slices and mint sprigs.
7. Serve your refreshing Cucumber Cooler Mocktail immediately.

PEACH BELLINI MOCKTAIL:

INGREDIENTS:

- 1 cup of peach puree (made from fresh or frOuncesen peaches)
- One tbsp of lemon juice
- Two tbsp of simple syrup
- 1 cup of sparkling water or ginger ale
- Crushed ice
- Peach slices for garnish

INSTRUCTIONS:

1. Combine the peach puree, lemon juice, and simple syrup in a blender.
2. Blend until smooth.

3. Fill a champagne flute or a tall glass halfway with the peach mixture.
4. Add crushed ice to fill up the glass.
5. Top it off with sparkling water or ginger ale.
6. Stir gently to mix the ingredients.
7. Garnish with a fresh peach slice.
8. Enjoy your delightful Peach Bellini Mocktail!

SPARKLING CRANBERRY LIMEADE:

INGREDIENTS:

- 1 cup of cranberry juice
- 1/2 cup of freshly squeezed lime juice
- Two tbsp simple syrup (adjust to taste)
- Sparkling water or club soda
- Ice cubes
- Fresh cranberries and lime slices for garnish

INSTRUCTIONS:

1. Combine the cranberry juice, freshly squeezed lime juice, and simple syrup in a pitcher.
2. Stir well to mix the ingredients.
3. Fill serving glasses with ice cubes.
4. Pour the cranberry-lime mixture over the ice, filling each glass about 2/3 full.
5. Top off the glasses with sparkling water or club soda.
6. Garnish with fresh cranberries and lime slices.
7. Stir gently and serve immediately.

RASPBERRY MINT FIZZ:

INGREDIENTS:

- 1 cup of fresh or fr0uncesen raspberries
- 8-10 fresh mint leaves
- One tbsp of honey or agave syrup (adjust to taste)
- One tbsp of freshly squeezed lemon juice
- Sparkling water or soda water
- Ice cubes
- Fresh raspberries and mint sprigs for garnish

INSTRUCTIONS:

1. Combine the raspberries, mint leaves, honey or agave syrup, and lemon juice in a blender.
2. Blend until smooth to make a raspberry-mint puree.
3. Fill serving glasses with ice cubes.
4. Pour the raspberry-mint puree into each glass, filling about 1/3 full.
5. Top off the glasses with sparkling water or soda water.
6. Stir gently to mix the flavors.
7. Garnish with fresh raspberries and mint sprigs.
8. Serve immediately.

COCONUT LIME MOCKTAIL:

INGREDIENTS:

- 1 cup of coconut water
- 1/2 cup of coconut milk
- Two tbsp of freshly squeezed lime juice
- One tbsp of simple syrup or maple syrup (adjust to taste)
- Ice cubes
- Lime slices and shredded coconut for garnish

INSTRUCTIONS:

a. Combine coconut water, coconut milk, freshly squeezed lime juice, and simple syrup in a shaker or a pitcher.
b. Shake or stir well to mix the ingredients.
c. Fill serving glasses with ice cubes.
d. Pour the coconut lime mixture over the ice, filling each glass 2/3.
e. Garnish with lime slices and a sprinkle of shredded coconut.
f. Stir gently and serve immediately.

KIWI SPARKLER:

INGREDIENTS:

- Two ripe kiwis, peeled and diced
- One tbsp of honey or agave syrup (adjust to taste)
- One tbsp of freshly squeezed lemon juice
- Sparkling water or club soda
- Ice cubes
- Kiwi slices for garnish

INSTRUCTIONS:

a. Blend the diced kiwis, honey or agave syrup, and lemon juice until smooth.
b. Fill serving glasses with ice cubes.
c. Pour the kiwi mixture into each glass, filling about 1/3 full.
d. Top off the drinks with sparkling water or club soda.
e. Stir gently to combine the flavors.
f. Garnish with kiwi slices.
g. Serve immediately.

MANGO-GINGER MOCKTAIL:

INGREDIENTS:

- 1 cup of fresh mango chunks (or frOuncesen mango, thawed)
- 1 tbsp freshly grated ginger
- One tbsp of honey or agave syrup (adjust to taste)
- 1 tbsp freshly squeezed lime juice
- Sparkling water or soda water
- Ice cubes
- Fresh mint leaves for garnish

INSTRUCTIONS:

a. Blend the mango chunks, freshly grated ginger, honey or agave syrup, and lime juice until smooth.
b. Fill serving glasses with ice cubes.
c. Pour the mango-ginger mixture into each glass, filling about 1/3 full.
d. Top off the glasses with sparkling water or soda water.
e. Stir gently to mix the flavors.
f. Garnish with fresh mint leaves.
g. Serve immediately.

BOOSTING BRAIN HEALTH WITH NUTRIBULLET:

BRAIN-BOOSTING BERRY BLAST:

INGREDIENTS:

- 1 cup of mixed berries (blueberries, strawberries, raspberries)

- One medium banana
- 1/2 cup of Greek yogurt
- One tbsp honey
- 1/2 cup of almond milk (or any milk of your choice)
- Ice cubes (optional)

INSTRUCTIONS:

a. Wash the berries thoroughly and remove any stems.
b. Peel the banana and cut it into smaller pieces.
c. Combine the mixed berries, banana, Greek yogurt, honey, and almond milk in a blender.
d. Blend until smooth and creamy.
e. Add a few ice cubes and blend again for a chilled smoothie if desired.
f. Pour the Brain-Boosting Berry Blast into a glass and enjoy!

WALNUT-BLUEBERRY BRAIN FUEL:

INGREDIENTS:

- 1 cup of fresh blueberries
- 1/2 cup of walnuts
- One tbsp of chia seeds
- 1 tsp honey (optional)
- 1/2 cup of Greek yogurt

INSTRUCTIONS:

a. Rinse the blueberries and drain them well.
b. In a food processor or blender, combine the blueberries, walnuts, chia seeds, Greek yogurt, and honey (if using).
c. Blend until you achieve a thick and creamy consistency.
d. Transfer the mixture to a bowl or glass and serve.

e. Optionally, you can sprinkle some additional walnuts and blueberries for extra flavor and presentation.

SPINACH AND FLAX MEMORY ENHANCER:

INGREDIENTS:

- 2 cups of fresh spinach leaves
- One ripe banana
- One tbsp of ground flaxseeds
- 1/2 cup of unsweetened almond milk
- 1/2 cup of orange juice

INSTRUCTIONS:

a. Thoroughly wash the spinach leaves and remove any tough stems.
b. Peel the banana and cut it into smaller chunks.
c. Combine the spinach, banana, ground flaxseeds, almond milk, and orange juice in a blender.
d. Blend until the mixture becomes smooth and homogeneous.
e. Pour the Spinach and Flax Memory Enhancer into a glass and enjoy this nutritious drink!

TURMERIC-GINGER COGNITIVE KICK:

INGREDIENTS:

- 1 cup of coconut milk
- 1/2 tsp ground turmeric
- 1/2 tsp grated fresh ginger
- One tbsp of honey or maple syrup (for sweetness)
- 1/4 tsp ground cinnamon (optional)

INSTRUCTIONS:

a. In a small saucepan, warm the coconut milk over low heat.
b. Add the ground turmeric and grated ginger to the coconut milk.
c. Stir in the honey or maple syrup and continue to heat until the mixture is well combined and slightly steaming.
d. Pour the Turmeric-Ginger Cognitive Kick into a mug.
e. If desired, sprinkle ground cinnamon for an extra flavor boost and antioxidants.
f. Enjoy this warm and comforting drink!

ALMOND AND DARK CHOCOLATE COGNITION ELIXIR:

INGREDIENTS:

- 1 cup of unsweetened almond milk
- 1 ounce dark chocolate (at least 70% cocoa), chopped
- 1/2 tsp pure vanilla extract
- One tsp of honey or agave syrup (optional for added sweetness)

INSTRUCTIONS:

a. In a saucepan, heat the almond milk over low to medium heat.
b. Add the chopped dark chocolate to the almond milk and stir until the chocolate is fully melted and incorporated.
c. Stir in the vanilla extract and honey (if using) until well combined.
d. Pour the Almond and Dark Chocolate Cognition Elixir into a mug.
e. Sip and enjoy this delightful and indulgent brain-boosting elixir!

KALE AND WALNUT NEURO-NOURISHER:

INGREDIENTS:

- 1 cup of kale leaves (washed and chopped)
- 1/2 cup of walnuts
- One ripe banana
- 1 cup of almond milk (or any other plant-based milk of your choice)
- 1 tbsp honey or maple syrup (optional for sweetness)
- Ice cubes (optional)

INSTRUCTIONS:

a. Add the chopped kale leaves, walnuts, and banana in a blender.
b. Pour in the almond milk and sweetener (if using).
c. Blend all the ingredients until smooth and creamy.
d. Add some ice cubes and blend again to chill the smoothie if desired.
e. Pour into a glass and enjoy your brain-nourishing kale and walnut smoothie.

F. AVOCADO BRAINPOWER SMOOTHIE:

INGREDIENTS:

- One ripe avocado
- 1 cup of spinach leaves (washed)
- 1/2 cup of blueberries (fresh or frOuncesen)
- One tbsp of almond butter
- 1 cup of coconut water
- One tsp of honey or agave syrup (optional for sweetness)

INSTRUCTIONS:

a. Peel the avocado, remove the pit, and place the flesh into a blender.
b. Add the spinach, blueberries, almond butter, and coconut water.
c. Optionally, add a sweetener like honey or agave syrup if desired.
d. Blend all the ingredients until you get a smooth and creamy consistency.
e. Pour the smoothie into a glass and serve immediately for a brain-boosting treat.

COCONUT-BERRY BRAIN BOOSTER:

INGREDIENTS:

- 1 cup of mixed berries (strawberries, blueberries, raspberries)
- 1/2 cup of Greek yogurt (or plant-based yogurt for a vegan option)
- 1/2 cup of coconut milk
- One tbsp flaxseeds
- One tsp of coconut oil
- 1 tsp honey or maple syrup (optional for sweetness)

INSTRUCTIONS:

a. Combine the mixed berries, Greek yogurt, coconut milk, flaxseeds, and coconut oil in a blender.
b. Optionally, add honey or maple syrup for extra sweetness.
c. Blend all the ingredients until the mixture is smooth and well combined.
d. Taste and adjust sweetness if needed.

e. Pour the coconut-berry brain booster into a glass and enjoy the brain-boosting goodness.

CHIA SEED OMEGA-3 SMOOTHIE:

INGREDIENTS:

- 1 cup of mixed berries (blueberries, strawberries, or raspberries)
- One tbsp of chia seeds
- 1 cup of unsweetened almond milk (or any other plant-based milk)
- One tbsp of almond butter
- One tsp of honey or agave syrup (optional for sweetness)
- Ice cubes (optional)

INSTRUCTIONS:

a. In a blender, add the mixed berries, chia seeds, almond milk, almond butter, and sweetener (if using).
b. Blend until all the ingredients are well combined and smooth.
c. Add some ice cubes and blend again to chill the smoothie if desired.
d. Pour into a glass and enjoy the omega-3-rich chia seed smoothie.

PUMPKIN SEED BRAIN BLEND:

INGREDIENTS:

- 1/2 cup of pumpkin seeds
- One ripe banana
- 1 cup of spinach leaves (washed)

- 1 cup of unsweetened soy milk (or any other plant-based milk)
- One tbsp of honey or maple syrup (optional for sweetness)
- A pinch of ground cinnamon (optional for flavor)

INSTRUCTIONS:

a. In a blender, combine the pumpkin seeds, ripe banana, spinach leaves, soy milk, and sweetener (if using).
b. Optionally, add a pinch of ground cinnamon for additional flavor.
c. Blend until you get a smooth and creamy consistency.
d. Taste and adjust sweetness if needed.
e. Pour the pumpkin seed brain blend into a glass and savor the nourishing goodness.

NUTRIBULLET FOR WEIGHT MANAGEMENT:

GREEN PROTEIN POWER SHAKE:

INGREDIENTS:

- 1 cup of unsweetened almond milk
- One ripe banana
- 1 cup of baby spinach leaves
- One scoop of vanilla protein powder (plant-based or whey, depending on your preference)
- One tbsp of chia seeds
- One tbsp of almond butter
- One tsp of honey (optional for added sweetness)

- Ice cubes (optional for a colder shake)

INSTRUCTIONS:

a. In a blender, combine the almond milk, banana, baby spinach, protein powder, chia seeds, almond butter, and honey (if using).
b. Blend quickly until all the ingredients are well combined and the shake is smooth and creamy.
c. Add some ice cubes and blend again if you prefer a colder shake.
d. Pour the Green Protein Power Shake into a glass and enjoy!

BERRY-BANANA WEIGHT LOSS SMOOTHIE:

INGREDIENTS:

- 1 cup of frOuncesen mixed berries (strawberries, blueberries, raspberries)
- One ripe banana
- 1 cup of unsweetened coconut water
- One tbsp of ground flaxseeds
- One tsp of honey (optional for added sweetness)

INSTRUCTIONS:

a. Place the frOuncesen mixed berries, ripe banana, coconut water, and ground flaxseeds in a blender.
b. Blend on high speed until the ingredients are well combined, and the smoothie has a creamy texture.
c. Taste the smoothie and add honey if you prefer a sweeter taste.
d. Blend again briefly to incorporate the honey.

e. Pour the Berry-Banana Weight Loss Smoothie into a glass and enjoy!

ALMOND BUTTER AND SPINACH SMOOTHIE:

INGREDIENTS:

- 1 cup of unsweetened almond milk
- 1 ripe banana
- 1 cup of fresh baby spinach leaves
- Two tbsp of almond butter
- One tbsp honey (optional for added sweetness)
- Ice cubes (optional for a colder smoothie)

INSTRUCTIONS:

a. Combine the almond milk, ripe banana, fresh baby spinach, almond butter, and honey (if using).
b. Blend quickly until all the ingredients are well blended and the smoothie is creamy.
c. Taste the smoothie and add more honey if you prefer it sweeter.
d. Add some ice cubes and blend again if you want a colder smoothie.
e. Pour the Almond Butter and Spinach Smoothie into a glass and enjoy!

CHIA SEED AND BERRY SLIMDOWN SHAKE:

INGREDIENTS:

- 1 cup of unsweetened almond milk
- 1/2 cup of frOuncesen mixed berries (blueberries, raspberries, strawberries)
- 1 tbsp chia seeds

- One tbsp of almond butter
- One tsp of honey (optional for added sweetness)
- A pinch of cinnamon (optional for extra flavor)

INSTRUCTIONS:

a. Combine the unsweetened almond milk, frOuncesen mixed berries, chia seeds, almond butter, honey (if using), and cinnamon (if desired) in a blender.
b. Blend quickly until the shake is smooth and all the ingredients are well combined.
c. Taste the shake and add more honey if you prefer it sweeter.
d. Pour the Chia Seed and Berry Slimdown Shake into a glass and enjoy!

AVOCADO AND KALE WEIGHT BUSTER:

INGREDIENTS:

- One ripe avocado, pitted and peeled
- 1 cup of fresh kale leaves (stems removed)
- 1 cup of unsweetened coconut water
- One tbsp of lemon juice
- One tbsp honey (optional for added sweetness)
- Ice cubes (optional for a colder shake)

INSTRUCTIONS:

a. Combine the ripe avocado, fresh kale leaves, coconut water, lemon juice, and honey (if using) in a blender.
b. Blend quickly until the shake is smooth and creamy and the ingredients thoroughly blend.
c. Taste the shake and add more honey if you prefer it sweeter.

d. For a colder shake, add some ice cubes and blend again.
e. Pour the Avocado and Kale Weight Buster into a glass and enjoy!

SPECIAL DIETARY CONSIDERATIONS: GLUTEN-FREE, VEGAN, ETC.:

QUINOA AND ROASTED VEGETABLE SALAD (GLUTEN-FREE, VEGAN):

INGREDIENTS:

- 1 cup of quinoa, rinsed
- 2 cups of mixed vegetables (bell peppers, cherry tomatoes, zucchini, etc.), chopped
- Two tbsp of olive oil
- One tsp of dried herbs (oregano, thyme, or rosemary)
- Salt and pepper, to taste
- 1/4 cup of chopped fresh parsley or cilantro
- Juice of 1 lemon
- 1/4 cup of chopped nuts (e.g., almonds or walnuts) (optional)

INSTRUCTIONS:

a. Preheat the oven to 400°F (200°C).
b. Toss the chopped vegetables in a bowl with one tbsp of olive oil, dried herbs, salt, and pepper.

c. Spread the vegetables on a baking sheet and roast them in the oven for 20-25 minutes or until tender and slightly caramelized.
d. Combine the quinoa with 2 cups of water and a pinch of salt in a medium saucepan. Please bring it to a boil, then reduce the heat, cover, and simmer for about 15 minutes or until the quinoa is cooked and the water is absorbed.
e. Combine the cooked quinoa with the roasted vegetables in a large mixing bowl.
f. Drizzle the remaining tbsp of olive oil and lemon juice over the salad. Toss everything together until well combined.
g. Garnish the salad with chopped fresh parsley or cilantro and chopped nuts (if using).
h. Serve warm or cold as a delicious gluten-free and vegan salad.

CAULIFLOWER RICE STIR-FRY (GLUTEN-FREE, VEGAN):

INGREDIENTS:

- One medium head of cauliflower, grated or pulsed into a rice-like texture
- 1 cup of mixed vegetables (carrots, peas, corn, broccoli, etc.)
- Two tbsp soy sauce (gluten-free tamari for a GF option)
- One tbsp of sesame oil
- One tbsp of olive oil
- Two garlic cloves minced
- One tsp of grated fresh ginger
- Salt and pepper, to taste
- Green onions, sliced, for garnish

INSTRUCTIONS:

a. Heat the olive oil and sesame oil over medium heat in a large skillet or wok.
b. Add minced garlic and grated ginger to the hot oil. Stir-fry for about 30 seconds until fragrant.
c. Add the mixed vegetables to the skillet and stir-fry for 3-4 minutes until they soften.
d. Add the cauliflower rice to the skillet, along with the soy sauce. Stir-fry everything together for another 4-5 minutes, allowing the cauliflower to cook and absorb the flavors.
e. Season with salt and pepper to taste.
f. Garnish with sliced green onions and serve immediately as a delicious gluten-free and vegan cauliflower rice stir-fry.

CHICKPEA AND VEGETABLE CURRY (GLUTEN-FREE, VEGAN):

INGREDIENTS:

- One can (15 Ounces) chickpeas, drained and rinsed
- 1 cup of mixed vegetables (bell peppers, peas, carrots, etc.)
- One can (14 Ounces) coconut milk
- One tbsp of curry powder
- One tsp of ground cumin
- One tsp of ground coriander
- 1/2 tsp turmeric
- One tbsp of vegetable oil
- One onion, chopped
- Two garlic cloves minced

- 1-inch piece of fresh ginger, grated
- Salt and pepper, to taste
- Fresh cilantro, chopped, for garnish

INSTRUCTIONS:

a. Heat the vegetable oil over medium heat in a large skillet or pot.
b. Add chopped onion, minced garlic, and grated ginger. Sauté until the onion becomes translucent and the mixture is aromatic.
c. Add the mixed vegetables to the skillet and sauté for a few minutes until they soften.
d. Stir in the curry powder, ground cumin, coriander, and turmeric. Cook for another minute to toast the spices.
e. Pour in the coconut milk and bring the mixture to a simmer.
f. Add the chickpeas to the skillet and let the curry simmer for 10-15 minutes, allowing the flavors to meld and the vegetables to cook through.
g. Season with salt and pepper to taste.
h. Garnish with chopped fresh cilantro, and serve the chickpea and vegetable curry with rice or gluten-free bread.

ZUCCHINI NOODLES WITH AVOCADO PESTO (GLUTEN-FREE, VEGAN):

INGREDIENTS:

- Three medium zucchinis, spiralized or thinly sliced
- One ripe avocado
- 1 cup of fresh basil leaves
- 1/4 cup of pine nuts or walnuts

- Two garlic cloves
- Two tbsp of lemon juice
- Three tbsp olive oil
- Salt and pepper, to taste
- Cherry tomatoes, halved, for garnish

INSTRUCTIONS:

a. Combine the ripe avocado, fresh basil, pine nuts or walnuts, minced garlic, lemon juice, olive oil, salt, and pepper in a blender or food processor.
b. Blend the ingredients until you get a smooth and creamy pesto sauce. If needed, add a little water to reach your desired consistency.
c. In a large bowl, toss the zucchini noodles with the avocado pesto until the noodles are evenly coated.
d. Garnish the dish with halved cherry tomatoes and additional basil leaves.
e. Serve the zucchini noodles with avocado pesto as a refreshing, satisfying gluten-free, vegan meal.

LENTIL AND SPINACH SOUP (GLUTEN-FREE, VEGAN):

INGREDIENTS:

- 1 cup of dried lentils (red or green), rinsed
- One onion, chopped
- Two garlic cloves minced
- One carrot, diced
- One celery stalk, diced
- 4 cups of vegetable broth
- One can (14 Ounces) diced tomatoes
- 2 cups of fresh spinach leaves

- One tsp of ground cumin
- One tsp of ground coriander
- 1/2 tsp paprika
- One tbsp of olive oil
- Salt and pepper, to taste
- Fresh parsley, chopped, for garnish

INSTRUCTIONS:

a. In a large pot, heat the olive oil over medium heat.
b. Add chopped onion, minced garlic, diced carrot, and diced celery. Sauté until the vegetables become tender and fragrant.
c. Stir in the ground cumin, ground coriander, and paprika. Cook for another minute to enhance the flavors.
d. Add the dried lentils to the pot, followed by the vegetable broth and diced tomatoes (with their juice). Bring the mixture to a boil.
e. Reduce the heat, cover the pot, and let the soup simmer for about 20-25 minutes or until the lentils are fully cooked and tender.
f. Stir in the fresh spinach leaves and let them wilt in the soup.
g. Season with salt and pepper to taste.
h. Garnish with chopped fresh parsley and serve the lentil and spinach soup as a comforting, hearty, gluten-free, vegan dish.

PORTOBELLO MUSHROOM BURGER (GLUTEN-FREE, VEGAN):

INGREDIENTS:

- Four large portobello mushroom caps

- 1/4 cup of balsamic vinegar
- Two tbsp of olive oil
- Two cloves garlic, minced
- One tsp of dried oregano
- Salt and pepper to taste
- Four gluten-free burger buns
- Lettuce leaves, sliced tomatoes, sliced red onions, and avocado slices (for toppings)

INSTRUCTIONS:

a. Clean the portobello mushroom caps and remove the stems.
b. Mix balsamic vinegar, olive oil, minced garlic, dried oregano, salt, and pepper in a bowl to make the marinade.
c. Place the portobello mushroom caps in a shallow dish and pour the marinade over them. Let them marinate for about 30 minutes, turning occasionally.
d. Preheat the grill or a grill pan over medium heat. Grill the marinated mushrooms for about 4-5 minutes per side or until tender.
e. Toast the gluten-free burger buns on the grill for a minute or until lightly browned.
f. Assemble the burger by placing a grilled mushroom cap on each bun. Add lettuce, tomato slices, red onion slices, and avocado slices as desired.
g. Serve the Portobello Mushroom Burgers with your favorite condiments and side dishes.

VEGAN PAD THAI WITH TOFU (GLUTEN-FREE, VEGAN):

INGREDIENTS:

- 8 Ounces rice noodles (gluten-free)
- 1 cup of firm tofu, cubed
- Two tbsp of vegetable oil
- 1/4 cup of tamari or soy sauce (gluten-free)
- Two tbsp tamarind paste
- Two tbsp maple syrup or brown sugar
- One tbsp of lime juice
- Two cloves garlic, minced
- 1 cup of bean sprouts
- 1 cup of shredded carrots
- 1/2 cup of sliced green onions
- 1/4 cup of chopped peanuts
- Fresh cilantro and lime wedges for garnish

INSTRUCTIONS:

a. Cook the rice noodles according to the package instructions. Drain and set aside.
b. Whisk together tamari or soy sauce, tamarind paste, maple syrup or brown sugar, and lime juice to make the sauce in a small bowl. Set aside.
c. Heat vegetable oil in a large skillet or wok over medium-high heat. Add the cubed tofu and stir-fry until lightly browned on all sides. Remove the tofu from the pan and set aside.
d. Add minced garlic, bean sprouts, shredded carrots, and sliced green onions in the same pan. Stir-fry for a couple of minutes until the vegetables are slightly tender.
e. Add the cooked rice noodles and the prepared sauce to the pan. Toss everything together until the noodles are coated with the sauce and heated through.
f. Add the stir-fried tofu back to the pan and toss to combine.

g. Serve the Vegan Pad Thai with tofu garnished with chopped peanuts, fresh cilantro, and lime wedges.

SPINACH AND ARTICHOKE QUINOA BITES (GLUTEN-FREE, VEGAN):

INGREDIENTS:

- 1 cup of cooked quinoa
- 1 cup of chopped spinach (fresh or frOuncesen)
- 1 cup of artichoke hearts, drained and chopped
- 1/2 cup of cooked and mashed sweet potato
- 1/4 cup of nutritional yeast (optional but adds a cheesy flavor)
- Two tbsp ground flaxseed mixed with five tbsp water (flax egg)
- Two cloves garlic, minced
- 1/2 tsp onion powder
- 1/2 tsp dried thyme
- Salt and pepper to taste
- Olive oil (for brushing)

INSTRUCTIONS:

a. Preheat your oven to 375°F (190°C) and line a baking sheet with parchment paper.
b. In a large mixing bowl, combine cooked quinoa, chopped spinach, chopped artichoke hearts, mashed sweet potato, nutritional yeast, flax egg, minced garlic, onion powder, dried thyme, salt, and pepper. Mix well until everything is evenly combined.
c. Take about 1-2 tbsp of the mixture and shape it into small, round bites. Place them on the prepared baking sheet.

d. Brush the tops of the quinoa bites with olive oil to help them get crispy in the oven.
   e. Bake the quinoa bites for about 20-25 minutes or until golden brown and firm to the touch.
   f. Remove from the oven and let them cool slightly before serving.

MEXICAN STUFFED BELL PEPPERS (GLUTEN-FREE, VEGAN):

INGREDIENTS:

- 4 large bell peppers (any color)
- 1 cup of cooked black beans
- 1 cup of cooked quinoa
- 1 cup of corn kernels (fresh, canned, or frOuncesen)
- 1 cup of diced tomatoes
- 1/2 cup of diced red onion
- 1/2 cup of diced zucchini
- 1/2 cup of diced red bell pepper
- Two cloves garlic, minced
- One tsp of ground cumin
- One tsp of chili powder
- Salt and pepper to taste
- Vegan shredded cheese (optional for topping)
- Fresh cilantro and lime wedges for garnish

INSTRUCTIONS:

   a. Preheat your oven to 375°F (190°C) and prepare a baking dish.
   b. Cut the tops off the bell peppers and remove the seeds and membranes.

c. In a large mixing bowl, combine cooked black beans, cooked quinoa, corn kernels, diced tomatoes, diced red onion, diced zucchini, diced red bell pepper, minced garlic, ground cumin, chili powder, salt, and pepper. Mix well until everything is evenly combined.
d. Stuff the mixture into each bell pepper, pressing down gently to pack it in.
e. Place the stuffed bell peppers in the prepared baking dish.
f. If using vegan shredded cheese, sprinkle some on each stuffed bell pepper.
g. Cover the baking dish with aluminum foil and bake for about 25-30 minutes or until the bell peppers are tender.
h. Remove the foil and bake for 5 minutes to melt the cheese (if using).
i. Garnish with fresh cilantro, and serve the Mexican Stuffed Bell Peppers with lime wedges.

Coconut Chia Seed Pudding (Gluten-Free, Vegan):

INGREDIENTS:

- 1/4 cup of chia seeds
- 1 cup of coconut milk (full-fat for creamier pudding)
- One tbsp of maple syrup or agave syrup
- 1/2 tsp vanilla extract
- Fresh fruits (e.g., berries, sliced bananas, mango) for topping
- Shredded coconut or chopped nuts (optional, for garnish)

INSTRUCTIONS:

a. Mix chia seeds, coconut milk, maple syrup or agave syrup, and vanilla extract in a bowl.

b. Stir well until all the ingredients are thoroughly combined.
c. Cover the bowl and refrigerate the mixture for at least 4 hours or overnight to allow the chia seeds to absorb the liquid and thicken into a pudding-like consistency.
d. Before serving, give the pudding a good stir to ensure no clumps.
e. Divide the Coconut Chia Seed Pudding into serving bowls or glasses.
f. Top with your favorite fresh fruits and shredded coconut or chopped nuts for added texture and flavor.

NUTRIBULLET RECIPES FOR KIDS:

BANANA-BERRY BLAST SMOOTHIE:

INGREDIENTS:

- One ripe banana
- 1 cup of mixed berries (such as strawberries, blueberries, and raspberries)
- 1 cup of spinach leaves
- 1/2 cup of Greek yogurt
- 1 cup of milk (dairy or plant-based)
- One tbsp honey (optional for added sweetness)

INSTRUCTIONS:

a. Peel the ripe banana and add it to a blender.
b. Add the mixed berries, spinach leaves, Greek yogurt, and milk to the blender.
c. Optionally, add honey for extra sweetness.
d. Blend all the ingredients until smooth and creamy.
e. Pour the smoothie into glasses and serve immediately.

HIDDEN VEGGIE TOMATO SAUCE:

INGREDIENTS:

- 1 can (28 Ounces) crushed tomatoes
- 1/2 cup of grated carrots
- 1/2 cup of grated zucchini
- 1/2 cup of finely chopped onions
- Two cloves garlic, minced
- Two tbsp of olive oil
- One tsp of dried basil
- One tsp of dried oregano
- Salt and pepper to taste

INSTRUCTIONS:

a. In a large saucepan, heat the olive oil over medium heat.
b. Add the minced garlic and chopped onions to the pan. Cook until the onions become translucent.
c. Stir in the grated carrots and zucchini. Cook for a few minutes until they soften.
d. Add the crushed tomatoes, dried basil, oregano, salt, and pepper to the pan. Stir everything together.
e. Reduce the heat to low and let the sauce simmer for 15-20 minutes, allowing the flavors to meld.
f. Taste and adjust seasoning as needed.
g. Use the sauce for pasta dishes, pizza, or as a dip.

CHEESY CAULIFLOWER TOTS:

INGREDIENTS:

- 2 cups of cauliflower florets
- 1 cup of shredded cheddar cheese
- 1/4 cup of grated Parmesan cheese

- One large egg, beaten
- 1/4 cup of breadcrumbs
- 1/2 tsp garlic powder
- 1/2 tsp onion powder
- Salt and pepper to taste
- Cooking spray or oil for greasing

INSTRUCTIONS:

Preheat your oven to 400°F (200°C) and grease a baking sheet with cooking spray or oil.

a. Steam the cauliflower florets until they become tender. Let them cool, then chop them finely or pulse them in a food processor.
b. Combine the chopped cauliflower, shredded cheddar cheese, grated Parmesan cheese, beaten egg, breadcrumbs, garlic powder, onion powder, salt, and pepper in a mixing bowl. Mix until well combined.
c. Take a tbsp of the mixture and shape it into a tot. Place it on the greased baking sheet. Repeat with the remaining mixture.
d. Bake the tots in the oven for about 15-20 minutes or until they become golden and crispy.
e. Serve the cheesy cauliflower tots as a tasty snack or a side dish.

APPLE CINNAMON OATMEAL BITES:

INGREDIENTS:

- 2 cups of rolled oats
- Two ripe bananas, mashed
- 1 cup of unsweetened applesauce

- 1/4 cup of honey or maple syrup
- One tsp of ground cinnamon
- 1/2 tsp vanilla extract
- 1/2 cup of chopped dried apples or raisins (optional)

INSTRUCTIONS:

a. Preheat your oven to 350°F (175°C) and line a baking sheet with parchment paper.
b. Combine the mashed bananas, unsweetened applesauce, honey (or maple syrup), ground cinnamon, and vanilla extract in a large mixing bowl. Mix until well combined.
c. Stir in the rolled oats and chopped dried apples or raisins (if using) until everything is evenly incorporated.
d. Drop spoonfuls of the mixture onto the prepared baking sheet, shaping them into bite-sized cookies.
e. Bake the oatmeal bites in the oven for 15-20 minutes or until they become firm and lightly golden.
f. Allow the bites to cool before serving. Store any leftovers in an airtight container.

GREEN MONSTER POPSICLES (WITH SPINACH AND FRUIT):

INGREDIENTS:

- 2 cups of fresh spinach leaves
- 1 cup of chopped pineapple
- 1 cup of chopped mango
- One ripe banana
- 1/2 cup of Greek yogurt
- 1/4 cup of orange juice
- One tbsp honey (optional for added sweetness)

INSTRUCTIONS:

a. In a blender, combine the fresh spinach leaves, chopped pineapple, chopped mango, ripe banana, Greek yogurt, orange juice, and honey (if using).
b. Blend all the ingredients until you get a smooth and creamy mixture.
c. Pour the green smoothie mixture into popsicle molds.
d. Insert popsicle sticks into the molds and freeze for at least 4 hours or until the popsicles are completely frOuncesen.
e. Once frOuncesen, remove the popsicles from the molds and enjoy these healthy and refreshing treats!

MINI VEGGIE FRITTATAS:

INGREDIENTS:

- Six large eggs
- 1/4 cup of milk
- 1/2 cup of diced bell peppers (assorted colors)
- 1/2 cup of diced tomatoes
- 1/2 cup of chopped spinach
- 1/4 cup of diced onions
- 1/4 cup of shredded cheddar cheese
- Salt and pepper to taste
- Cooking spray or muffin liners

INSTRUCTIONS:

a. Preheat your oven to 375°F (190°C). Grease a muffin tin with cooking spray or line it with muffin liners.

b. In a bowl, whisk together the eggs and milk until well combined.
c. Stir in the diced bell peppers, tomatoes, chopped spinach, onions, shredded cheddar cheese, salt, and pepper. Mix until all the ingredients are evenly distributed.
d. Pour the egg mixture into each muffin cup of, filling them about 2/3 of the way.
e. Bake in the oven for 15-18 minutes or until the frittatas are set and slightly golden on top.
f. Remove from the oven and let them cool for a few minutes before serving.

PEANUT BUTTER AND JELLY SMOOTHIE:

INGREDIENTS:

- 1 cup of frOuncesen mixed berries (strawberries, blueberries, raspberries)
- One ripe banana
- Two tbsp of peanut butter
- 1 cup of milk (dairy or plant-based)
- One tbsp honey (optional for added sweetness)
- Ice cubes (optional if you prefer a thicker smoothie)

INSTRUCTIONS:

a. In a blender, combine the frOuncesen mixed berries, ripe banana, peanut butter, milk, and honey (if using).
b. Blend on high speed until all the ingredients are well combined, and the smoothie is creamy and smooth.
c. Add a few ice cubes and blend again if you prefer a thicker consistency.

d. Pour the smoothie into glasses and serve immediately. If desired, you can garnish with a few extra berries or a peanut butter drizzle.

SWEET POTATO FRIES WITH DIPPING SAUCE:

INGREDIENTS:

- Two large sweet potatoes peeled and cut into thin strips
- Two tbsp of olive oil
- One tsp paprika
- 1/2 tsp garlic powder
- 1/2 tsp salt
- 1/4 tsp black pepper
- For the dipping sauce:
- 1/4 cup of mayonnaise
- One tbsp ketchup
- One tsp honey
- 1/2 tsp Dijon mustard
- Pinch of salt and pepper

INSTRUCTIONS:

a. Preheat your oven to 425°F (220°C) and line a baking sheet with parchment paper.
b. Toss the sweet potato strips with olive oil, paprika, garlic powder, salt, and black pepper in a large bowl until they are well coated.
c. Spread the sweet potato strips in a single layer on the prepared baking sheet, ensuring they are not overcrowded.
d. Bake in the preheated oven for about 20-25 minutes, flipping halfway through or until the sweet potato fries are crispy and golden.

e. While the fries are baking, prepare the dipping sauce by mixing all the sauce ingredients in a small bowl until smooth.
f. Once the sweet potato fries are ready, serve them hot with the dipping sauce on the side.

VEGGIE RAINBOW WRAPS WITH HUMMUS:

INGREDIENTS:

- Sizeable whole wheat or spinach tortillas
- 1 cup of hummus (store-bought or homemade)
- Assorted colorful veggies (carrots, bell peppers, cucumbers, avocado, red cabbage, etc.), julienned or thinly sliced

INSTRUCTIONS:

a. Lay the whole wheat or spinach tortillas on a clean surface.
b. Spread a generous layer of hummus over the entire surface of each tortilla.
c. Place the julienned or thinly sliced veggies in a line down the center of each tortilla.
d. Carefully fold the sides of the tortilla over the veggies, then roll it up tightly to form a wrap.
e. Slice the wraps in half diagonally and serve immediately. You can also wrap them in parchment paper for easier handling.

STRAWBERRY-BANANA FROUNCESEN YOGURT BITES:

INGREDIENTS:

- 1 cup of strawberries, washed and hulled
- One ripe banana
- 1 cup of plain Greek yogurt
- Two tbsp honey (optional for added sweetness)

INSTRUCTIONS:

a. In a blender or food processor, combine the strawberries, banana, Greek yogurt, and honey (if using).
b. Blend until the mixture is smooth and creamy.
c. Spoon the yogurt mixture into silicone ice cube trays or small cup ofcake liners on a baking sheet.
d. Freeze the yogurt bites for at least 2-3 hours or until they are firm.
e. Once frOuncesen, pop the yogurt bites out of the ice cube trays or cup ofcake liners and transfer them to an airtight container or resealable plastic bag for storage in the freezer.

ANTI-INFLAMMATORY BLENDS:

TURMERIC AND GINGER IMMUNITY SHOT:

INGREDIENTS:

- 1-inch piece of fresh turmeric root (or one tsp of turmeric powder)
- 1-inch piece of fresh ginger root
- One tbsp of honey (or maple syrup for a vegan option)
- Juice of half a lemon
- A pinch of black pepper
- 1/2 cup of water

INSTRUCTIONS:

a. Wash and peel the turmeric and ginger roots.
b. Combine the turmeric, ginger, honey, lemon juice, black pepper, and water in a blender or juicer.
c. Blend or juice until everything is well combined.
d. Strain the mixture through a fine-mesh sieve to remove any solids.
e. Pour the liquid into a shot glass and consume immediately.

PINEAPPLE-TURMERIC SMOOTHIE:

INGREDIENTS:

- 1 cup of pineapple chunks (fresh or fr0uncesen)
- 1/2 banana
- 1/2 cup of coconut milk (or any other milk of your choice)
- 1/2 tsp turmeric powder
- One tbsp of chia seeds
- Ice cubes (if using fresh pineapple)

INSTRUCTIONS:

a. Add pineapple chunks, banana, coconut milk, turmeric powder, and chia seeds in a blender.
b. Blend until you get a smooth and creamy consistency.
c. If using fresh pineapple, add a few ice cubes and blend until chilled.
d. Pour the smoothie into a glass and serve immediately.

MANGO-TURMERIC LASSI:

INGREDIENTS:

- 1 cup of ripe mango chunks
- 1/2 cup of plain yogurt
- 1/2 cup of water
- 1/2 tsp turmeric powder
- One tbsp honey (adjust to taste)

INSTRUCTIONS:

a. Combine the mango chunks, yogurt, water, turmeric powder, and honey in a blender.
b. Blend until everything is well combined, and you have a smooth mixture.
c. Taste and adjust sweetness if needed by adding more honey.
d. Pour the lassi into glasses and serve chilled.

GOLDEN MILK ELIXIR:

INGREDIENTS:

- 1 cup of milk (dairy or plant-based)
- One tsp of turmeric powder
- 1/2 tsp cinnamon powder
- 1/4 tsp ground ginger
- One tbsp of honey (or maple syrup for a vegan option)
- A pinch of black pepper

INSTRUCTIONS:

a. In a small saucepan, heat the milk over medium-low heat.
b. Add the turmeric powder, cinnamon powder, ground ginger, honey, and black pepper.
c. Whisk everything together and continue heating until the mixture is hot but not boiling.
d. Pour the golden milk into a mug and enjoy.

GREEN TEA AND BERRY ANTIOXIDANT BLEND:

INGREDIENTS:

- 1 cup of brewed green tea, cooled
- 1/2 cup of mixed berries (strawberries, blueberries, raspberries, etc.)
- One tbsp honey (adjust to taste)
- Ice cubes (optional)

INSTRUCTIONS:

a. Combine the brewed green tea, mixed berries, and honey in a blender.
b. Blend until you get a smooth and vibrant mixture.
c. Add some ice cubes and blend again to chill the blend.
d. Pour the antioxidant blend into glasses and serve immediately.

BLUEBERRY-GINGER ANTI-INFLAMMATORY SMOOTHIE:

INGREDIENTS:

- 1 cup of blueberries (fresh or frOuncesen)
- One small piece of ginger (about 1 inch), peeled and grated
- 1 cup of spinach leaves
- One tbsp of chia seeds
- 1 cup of almond milk (or any other milk of your choice)
- One tbsp of honey or maple syrup (optional for sweetness)
- Ice cubes (optional)

INSTRUCTIONS:

a. Add the blueberries, grated ginger, spinach, chia seeds, and almond milk in a blender.
b. Optionally, add honey or maple syrup for sweetness, if desired.
c. Blend all the ingredients until smooth and creamy.
d. Add some ice cubes and blend again if you prefer a colder smoothie.
e. Pour the smoothie into a glass and enjoy its anti-inflammatory goodness!

KALE AND PINEAPPLE ANTI-INFLAMMATORY JUICE:

INGREDIENTS:

- 2 cups of kale leaves (stems removed)
- 1 cup of fresh pineapple chunks
- One cucumber (peeled if desired)
- One lemon (peeled)
- 1-inch piece of fresh turmeric root (or one tsp of turmeric powder)
- 1 cup of water or coconut water

INSTRUCTIONS:

a. Wash all the fruits and vegetables thoroughly.
b. Cut the kale leaves, pineapple, cucumber, and lemon into chunks for easy blending.
c. Peel and grate the fresh turmeric root.
d. Add the kale, pineapple, cucumber, lemon, and turmeric in a juicer or high-speed blender.
e. Add the water or coconut water for a smoother consistency.

f. Blend or juice all the ingredients until you get a smooth, refreshing juice.
g. Using a blender, strain the liquid through a fine mesh strainer to remove any pulp.
h. Pour the liquid into a glass and enjoy the anti-inflammatory benefits of this green elixir.

PAPAYA AND TURMERIC DIGESTIVE SOOTHER:

INGREDIENTS:

- 1 cup of ripe papaya (peeled, seeds removed, and chopped)
- 1-inch piece of fresh turmeric root (or one tsp of turmeric powder)
- One tbsp of fresh lemon juice
- One tbsp honey
- 1 cup of coconut water (or regular water)

INSTRUCTIONS:

a. Combine the ripe papaya chunks, fresh turmeric, lemon juice, honey, and coconut water in a blender.
b. Blend all the ingredients until you achieve a smooth and creamy consistency.
c. Taste the mixture and adjust the sweetness with more honey if desired.
d. Pour the digestive soother into a glass and savor its soothing and anti-inflammatory properties.

CUCUMBER AND ALOE VERA COOLER:

INGREDIENTS:

- One large cucumber (peeled and chopped)

- 1 cup of aloe vera gel (freshly extracted, if possible)
- One tbsp of fresh lime juice
- One tbsp of mint leaves (optional for added freshness)
- 1 cup of water or coconut water
- Ice cubes (optional)

INSTRUCTIONS:

a. Add the chopped cucumber, aloe vera gel, lime juice, and mint leaves (if using) in a blender.
b. Blend the ingredients until they form a smooth and cooling mixture.
c. Add water or coconut water to adjust the consistency as per your preference.
d. If you like it chilled, add some ice cubes and blend again.
e. Pour the cucumber and aloe vera cooler into a glass and enjoy its hydrating and anti-inflammatory benefits.

SPINACH AND CHERRY INFLAMMATION BUSTER:

INGREDIENTS:

- 1 cup of fresh or frOuncesen cherries (pitted)
- 1 cup of baby spinach leaves
- 1/2 banana
- One tbsp of almond butter
- 1 cup of almond milk (or any other milk of your choice)
- One tsp of honey (optional for sweetness)
- Ice cubes (optional)

INSTRUCTIONS:

a. Add the cherries, baby spinach, banana, almond butter, and almond milk in a blender.

b. Optionally, add honey for a touch of sweetness.
c. Blend all the ingredients until you get a creamy and delicious smoothie.
d. If you prefer colder, add some ice cubes and blend again.
e. Pour the spinach and cherry inflammation buster into a glass and enjoy the powerful anti-inflammatory combination.

BEAUTY FROM WITHIN: SMOOTHIES FOR RADIANT SKIN AND HAIR

BERRY BEAUTY BOOSTER:

INGREDIENTS:

- 1 cup of blueberries (fresh or fr0uncesen)
- 1 cup of strawberries (fresh or fr0uncesen)
- 1 cup of spinach leaves (fresh)
- 1 cup of almond milk
- One tbsp of chia seeds

INSTRUCTIONS:

1. Wash the blueberries, strawberries, and spinach thoroughly.
2. If using fresh fruit, remove the stems from the strawberries.
3. Add the blueberries, strawberries, spinach, almond milk, and chia seeds in a blender.
4. Blend on high speed until all the ingredients are smooth and well combined.

5. Add more almond milk to reach your desired consistency if the smoothie is too thick.
6. Pour the smoothie into a glass, and it's ready to enjoy!

GREEN GODDESS GLOW:

INGREDIENTS:

- 2 cups of kale leaves (stems removed)
- 1/2 cucumber (peeled and chopped)
- 1 cup of pineapple chunks (fresh or frOuncesen)
- 1/2 avocado (peeled and pitted)
- 1 cup of coconut water
- One tbsp flaxseed

INSTRUCTIONS:

1. Wash the kale leaves and cucumber thoroughly.
2. Add the kale, cucumber, pineapple, avocado, coconut water, and flaxseed in a blender.
3. Blend on high speed until all the ingredients are smooth and creamy.
4. Add more coconut water to adjust the consistency if the smoothie is too thick.
5. Pour the smoothie into a glass, ready to refresh and nourish you!

MANGO MELON MAGIC:

INGREDIENTS:

- One ripe mango (peeled and pitted)
- 1 cup of cantaloupe chunks (seeds removed)
- One medium-sized carrot (peeled and chopped)
- 1/2 cup of Greek yogurt

- One tbsp honey (adjust to taste)
- 1/2 tsp turmeric powder

INSTRUCTIONS:

1. Wash and peel the mango, cantaloupe, and carrot.
2. Add the mango, cantaloupe, carrot, Greek yogurt, honey, and turmeric powder in a blender.
3. Blend on high speed until all the ingredients are smooth and creamy.
4. Taste the smoothie and adjust the sweetness with more honey if desired.
5. Pour the smoothie into a glass, ready to enchant your taste buds!

CITRUS RADIANCE REFRESHER:

INGREDIENTS:

- Two oranges (peeled and segmented)
- One grapefruit (peeled and segmented)
- One lemon (peeled and segmented)
- 1-inch piece of fresh ginger (peeled and grated)
- 2 cups of diced watermelon (seeds removed)
- 5-6 fresh mint leaves
- 1/2 cup of water (optional for adjusting consistency)

INSTRUCTIONS:

1. Wash and peel the oranges, grapefruit, and lemon. Separate the segments and remove any seeds.
2. Add the orange, grapefruit, lemon, grated ginger, watermelon, and mint leaves in a blender.
3. Blend on high speed until all the ingredients are well combined, and the smoothie is smooth.
4. If the smoothie is too thick, add water to reach your desired consistency.
5. Pour the refreshing Citrus Radiance Refresher into a glass, garnish with mint leaves if desired, and enjoy!

POMEGRANATE PARADISE:

INGREDIENTS:

- 1/2 cup of pomegranate seeds
- 1 cup of fresh or fr0uncesen raspberries
- One small beet (peeled and chopped)
- 1 cup of coconut milk (or coconut water for a lighter version)
- 1 cup of spinach leaves (fresh)
- One tbsp honey (optional, adjust to taste)

INSTRUCTIONS:

1. Wash and peel the beet. Chop it into smaller pieces for more effortless blending.
2. In a blender, add the pomegranate seeds, raspberries, chopped beet, coconut milk, spinach, and honey (if using).
3. Blend on high speed until all the ingredients are well combined, and the smoothie is creamy.
4. Taste the smoothie and add more honey if you prefer it sweeter.

5. Pour the vibrant Pomegranate Paradise into a glass and savor the burst of flavors!

SILKY SILICA SMOOTHIE:

INGREDIENTS:

- 2 cups of spinach leaves (fresh)
- One ripe banana
- 1/2 cucumber (peeled and chopped)
- Two tbsp hemp seeds
- 1 cup of almond milk (or any milk of your choice)

INSTRUCTIONS:

1. Wash the spinach leaves and peel the cucumber.
2. Add the spinach, banana, cucumber, hemp seeds, and almond milk in a blender.
3. Blend on high speed until all the ingredients are smooth and creamy.
4. Add more almond milk to adjust the consistency if the smoothie is too thick.
5. Pour the nourishing Silky Silica Smoothie into a glass and enjoy its goodness!

BERRY GLOW RADIANCE

INGREDIENTS:

- 1 cup of mixed berries (strawberries, blueberries, raspberries, blackberries)
- 1/2 cup of Greek yogurt
- 1/2 cup of almond milk (or any milk of your choice)
- One tbsp of chia seeds
- One tsp of honey (optional)

- Ice cubes (optional)

INSTRUCTIONS:

1. Add all the ingredients to your Nutribullet or blender.
2. Blend until smooth and creamy.
3. Taste and adjust sweetness with honey if desired.
4. Pour into a glass, garnish with a few berries, and enjoy your berry glow radiance smoothie!

AVOCADO COLLAGEN BOOSTER

INGREDIENTS:

- One ripe avocado peeled and pitted
- 1 cup of spinach leaves
- 1/2 cup of cucumber, chopped
- 1/2 cup of pineapple chunks
- 1 cup of coconut water
- A squeeze of lime juice
- Ice cubes (optional)

INSTRUCTIONS:

1. Place all the ingredients into your Nutribullet or blender.
2. Blend until well combined and creamy.
3. Add more coconut water or water to reach your desired consistency if the smoothie is too thick.
4. Pour into a glass, add a lime slice for garnish, and enjoy your avocado collagen booster!

CARROT ORANGE RADIANCE

INGREDIENTS:

- Two large carrots, peeled and chopped

- One orange, peeled and segmented
- 1/2 inch fresh ginger, peeled
- 1/2 cup of coconut water
- One tbsp flaxseeds
- Ice cubes (optional)

INSTRUCTIONS:

1. Put all the ingredients into your Nutribullet or blender.
2. Blend until smooth and creamy.
3. Taste and add more ginger or honey for extra flavor if desired.
4. Pour into a glass, garnish with a carrot stick, and enjoy your carrot orange radiance smoothie!

SPINACH BLUEBERRY BEAUTY

INGREDIENTS:

- 2 cups of baby spinach
- 1 cup of blueberries (fresh or fr0uncesen)
- One ripe banana
- 1/2 cup of plain Greek yogurt
- One tbsp of almond butter
- 1 cup of almond milk (or any milk of your choice)
- Ice cubes (optional)

INSTRUCTIONS:

1. Add all the ingredients to your Nutribullet or blender.
2. Blend until well blended and creamy.
3. Add more almond milk to achieve your preferred consistency if the smoothie is too thick.
4. Pour into a glass, add a sprinkle of chia seeds, and enjoy your spinach blueberry beauty smoothie!

COCONUT CUCUMBER HYDRATOR

INGREDIENTS:

- 1 cup of chopped cucumber
- 1/2 cup of coconut water
- 1/2 cup of coconut milk
- One tbsp of fresh mint leaves
- One tbsp of lime juice
- A pinch of salt
- Ice cubes (optional)

INSTRUCTIONS:

1. Combine all the ingredients in your Nutribullet or blender.
2. Blend until smooth and refreshing.
3. Adjust the taste by adding more lime juice or mint leaves if desired.
4. Pour into a glass, garnish with a mint sprig, and enjoy your coconut cucumber hydrator!

ENERGIZING NUTRIBLASTS: BEAT THE AFTERNOON SLUMP

COFFEE KICKSTART:

INGREDIENTS:

- 1 cup of cold-brew coffee (or chilled brewed coffee)
- One ripe banana
- 1/4 cup of rolled oats
- Two tbsp of almond butter
- 3-4 dates (pitted)

INSTRUCTIONS:

1. Add the cold-brew coffee, ripe banana, rolled oats, almond butter, and pitted dates in a blender.
2. Blend on high speed until all the ingredients are well combined, and the smoothie is creamy.
3. Add more cold-brew coffee or almond milk if you prefer a thinner consistency.
4. Pour the Coffee Kickstart into a glass, ready to give you a delicious caffeine boost with added nutrients!

POWER-PACKED GREEN ENERGY:

INGREDIENTS:

- 2 cups of spinach leaves (fresh)
- Two ripe kiwis (peeled and chopped)
- 1 cup of pineapple chunks (fresh or frOuncesen)
- One tsp of matcha powder
- 1 cup of coconut water

INSTRUCTIONS:

1. Wash the spinach leaves thoroughly.
2. Add the spinach, chopped kiwis, pineapple chunks, matcha powder, and coconut water in a blender.
3. Blend on high speed until all the ingredients are smooth and well combined.
4. Taste the smoothie and add a little honey if you prefer it sweeter.
5. Pour the Power-packed Green Energy smoothie into a glass, ready to revitalize your day!

CHOCO-BANANA BOOST:

INGREDIENTS:

- Two tbsp of cocoa powder
- Two ripe bananas
- 1/2 cup of Greek yogurt
- One tbsp honey (adjust to taste)
- 1 cup of almond milk

INSTRUCTIONS:

1. Add cocoa powder, ripe bananas, Greek yogurt, honey, and almond milk in a blender.
2. Blend on high speed until all the ingredients are smooth and creamy.
3. Taste the smoothie and adjust the sweetness with more honey if desired.
4. Pour the Choco-Banana Boost into a glass, and it's ready to indulge your taste buds with a nutritious chocolate treat!

NUTTY PROTEIN PUNCH:

INGREDIENTS:

- Two tbsp of peanut butter
- One tbsp of hemp seeds
- 2 cups of spinach leaves (fresh)
- One ripe banana
- 1 cup of milk (dairy or plant-based)

INSTRUCTIONS:

1. Wash the spinach leaves thoroughly.
2. Add peanut butter, hemp seeds, spinach, ripe banana, and milk in a blender.

3. Blend on high speed until all the ingredients are well combined, and the smoothie is creamy.
4. If the smoothie is too thick, add more milk to reach your desired consistency.
5. Pour the Nutty Protein Punch into a glass to fuel you with plant-based protein and nutrients!

TROPICAL TURMERIC REFUEL:

INGREDIENTS:

- One ripe mango (peeled and pitted)
- One tsp of turmeric powder (or 1-inch piece of fresh turmeric, peeled)
- One tsp of grated ginger
- 1 cup of coconut milk
- One tbsp honey (adjust to taste)

INSTRUCTIONS:

1. Wash, peel, and pit the ripe mango.
2. Add the mango, turmeric powder or fresh turmeric, grated ginger, coconut milk, and honey in a blender.
3. Blend on high speed until all the ingredients are smooth and well combined.
4. Taste the smoothie and add more honey if you prefer it sweeter.
5. Pour the Tropical Turmeric Refuel into a glass, and it's ready to recharge your body with tropical goodness and the anti-inflammatory benefits of turmeric!

ENERGIZING ESPRESSO SHAKE:

INGREDIENTS:

- One shot of espresso (about 1 ounce) - cooled
- One fr0uncesen banana
- One scoop of vanilla protein powder
- 1 cup of almond milk (or any milk of your choice)
- 1 cup of ice cubes

INSTRUCTIONS:

1. Brew a shot of espresso and let it cool to room temperature.
2. Peel and freeze a ripe banana in advance.
3. Add the cooled espresso, fr0uncesen banana, vanilla protein powder, almond milk, and ice cubes in a blender.
4. Blend quickly until all the ingredients are well combined, and the shake is creamy.
5. Pour the Energizing Espresso Shake into a glass, and it's ready to give you a boost of energy with a delicious coffee flavor!

ESPRESSO PROTEIN BOOST:

INGREDIENTS:

- One shot of espresso (about 1-2 ounces)
- 1/2 cup of milk of your choice (dairy or plant-based)
- One scoop of chocolate or vanilla protein powder
- One tbsp of almond butter or peanut butter (optional for added creaminess and flavor)
- Ice cubes

INSTRUCTIONS:

1. Brew a shot of espresso and let it cool slightly.

2. In a blender, combine the espresso, milk, protein powder, and almond butter (if using).
3. Blend quickly until all the ingredients are well combined and smooth.
4. Add a few ice cubes to the blender and pulse until the drink is chilled.
5. Pour the Espresso Protein Boost into a glass and enjoy!

MATCHA ENERGY ELIXIR:

INGREDIENTS:

- One tsp of matcha green tea powder
- 1 cup of hot water (not boiling, around 175°F or 80°C)
- One tbsp of honey or maple syrup (adjust to taste)
- 1/2 cup of unsweetened almond milk or any milk of your choice
- Ice cubes

INSTRUCTIONS:

1. Whisk the matcha green tea powder with hot water in a cup of or bowl until fully dissolved.
1. Add honey or maple syrup to sweeten the mixture to your desired taste.
2. Let the matcha mixture cool to room temperature or refrigerate for a few minutes.
3. In a separate glass, add ice cubes and pour the almond milk over them.
4. Slowly pour the cooled matcha mixture over the almond milk.
5. Stir gently to combine the flavors, and your Matcha Energy Elixir is ready to enjoy!

CITRUS WAKE-UP CALL:

INGREDIENTS:

- 1 cup of freshly squeezed orange juice
- 1/2 cup of freshly squeezed grapefruit juice
- One tbsp of lemon juice
- One tbsp of honey or agave syrup (adjust to taste)
- Ice cubes
- Lemon or orange slices for garnish (optional)

INSTRUCTIONS:

1. Combine the orange, grapefruit, and lemon juice in a pitcher.
2. Stir in the honey or agave syrup until it's well incorporated and sweetened to your preference.
3. Fill a glass with ice cubes.
4. Pour the Citrus Wake-Up Call mixture over the ice.
5. Garnish with lemon or orange slices, and enjoy the refreshing citrusy drink!

CHIA SEED POWER-UP:

INGREDIENTS:

- 2 cups of unsweetened almond milk or any milk of your choice
- 1/4 cup of chia seeds
- One tbsp of honey or maple syrup (adjust to taste)
- 1/2 tsp vanilla extract
- Fresh berries or sliced fruits for topping (e.g., strawberries, blueberries, bananas)

INSTRUCTIONS:

1. Combine the almond milk, chia seeds, honey or maple syrup, and vanilla extract in a bowl or container with a lid.
2. Stir well to ensure the chia seeds are evenly distributed and not clumping together.
3. Cover the bowl or container and refrigerate for at least 4 hours or overnight to allow the chia seeds to absorb the liquid and create a gel-like consistency.
4. Once the mixture has thickened, could you give it a good stir?
5. Pour the Chia Seed Power Up into serving glasses or bowls.
6. Top with fresh berries or sliced fruits, and enjoy the nutritious and filling Chia Seed Power Up!

MANGO TANGO ZING:

INGREDIENTS:

- One ripe mango, peeled and diced
- 1/2 cup of orange juice
- 1/4 cup of plain yogurt or coconut yogurt for a dairy-free option
- One tbsp of honey or agave syrup (adjust to taste)
- 1/2 tsp grated fresh ginger
- Ice cubes
- Mint leaves for garnish (optional)

INSTRUCTIONS:

1. Combine the diced mango, orange juice, yogurt, honey, agave syrup, and grated ginger in a blender.
2. Blend on high speed until the mixture is smooth and creamy.

3. Taste and adjust sweetness if needed by adding more honey or agave syrup.
4. Fill glasses with ice cubes.
5. Pour the Mango Tango Zing mixture over the ice.
6. Garnish with mint leaves if desired, and savor the tropical flavors!

DESSERT-INSPIRED SMOOTHIES: GUILT-FREE INDULGENCE

CHOCOLATE-ALMOND DREAM:

INGREDIENTS:

- 1/4 cup of dark chocolate chips or chopped dark chocolate
- 1 cup of almond milk
- One ripe banana
- 2-3 dates (pitted)
- 1 cup of ice cubes

INSTRUCTIONS:

1. In a microwave-safe bowl, melt the dark chocolate in the microwave or over a double boiler until smooth.
2. Combine the melted chocolate, almond milk, ripe banana, pitted dates, and ice cubes in a blender.
3. Blend on high until the mixture is smooth and creamy.

4. Pour the Chocolate-Almond Dream into a glass, and you can optionally top it with some additional chocolate shavings or a drizzle of melted chocolate for garnish.
5. Enjoy this decadent and satisfying chocolatey treat!

BERRY CHEESECAKE DELIGHT:

INGREDIENTS:

- 1 cup of strawberries (fresh or frOuncesen)
- 4 Ounces cream cheese
- 1/2 cup of Greek yogurt
- One tbsp honey (adjust to taste)
- 2-3 graham crackers (for garnish)

INSTRUCTIONS:

1. Wash and hull the strawberries if using fresh ones.
2. Combine the strawberries, cream cheese, Greek yogurt, and honey in a blender.
3. Blend until the mixture is smooth and creamy.
4. Crush the graham crackers into fine crumbs.
5. Layer the strawberry cheesecake mixture with the crushed graham crackers in serving glasses or jars.
6. Repeat the layers until the glasses are filled.
7. Top with a fresh strawberry or a graham cracker crumb for decoration.
8. Refrigerate for at least 1 hour before serving to let the flavors meld together.
9. Enjoy this delightful and creamy Berry Cheesecake treat!

CARAMEL APPLE CRISP:

INGREDIENTS:

- One apple (peeled, cored, and chopped)
- 1/2 tsp ground cinnamon
- Two tbsp caramel sauce (store-bought or homemade)
- 1/4 cup of rolled oats
- 1/2 cup of almond milk

INSTRUCTIONS:

1. Preheat your oven to 375°F (190°C).
2. In a bowl, toss the chopped apple with the ground cinnamon until evenly coated.
3. Drizzle half of the caramel sauce over the apples and mix well.
4. Transfer the caramel-coated apples to a small baking dish.
5. Combine the rolled oats with the almond milk and the remaining caramel sauce in a separate bowl.
6. Stir until the oats are evenly coated.
7. Pour the oat mixture over the apples in the baking dish.
8. Bake in the oven for about 20-25 minutes or until the apples are tender and the oat topping is golden and crispy.
9. Remove from the oven and let it cool slightly before serving.
10. Serve warm, and add a scoop of vanilla ice cream or a dollop of whipped cream for extra indulgence.
11. Enjoy this comforting and sweet Caramel Apple Crisp!

MINT CHOCOLATE CHIP BLISS:

INGREDIENTS:

- Handful of spinach
- 6-8 fresh mint leaves

- One tbsp of cacao nibs or dark chocolate chips
- One ripe banana
- 1 cup of coconut milk (or any milk of your choice)
- 1 cup of ice cubes

INSTRUCTIONS:

1. Wash the spinach and mint leaves thoroughly.
2. Combine the spinach, fresh mint leaves, cacao nibs (or dark chocolate chips), ripe banana, coconut milk, and ice cubes in a blender.
3. Blend on high until the mixture is smooth and creamy.
4. Pour the Mint Chocolate Chip Bliss into a glass, and you can optionally sprinkle some additional cacao nibs or dark chocolate chips on top for garnish.
5. Sip and enjoy this refreshing and nutritious minty treat!

PEACH COBBLER CONCOCTION:

INGREDIENTS:

- Two ripe peaches (peeled, pitted, and chopped)
- 1/2 tsp vanilla extract
- 1/4 cup of rolled oats
- 1/2 cup of Greek yogurt
- 1 cup of almond milk

INSTRUCTIONS:

1. Combine the chopped peaches, vanilla extract, rolled oats, Greek yogurt, and almond milk in a blender.
2. Blend until the mixture is smooth and well combined.
3. Pour the Peach Cobbler Concoction into a glass, and add a peach slice or a sprinkle of oats on top for decoration.
4. Enjoy this delightful and peachy treat!

LEMON-BLUEBERRY PIE:

INGREDIENTS:

- Juice of 1 lemon
- 1 cup of blueberries (fresh or fr0uncesen)
- 1/4 cup of cashews (soaked in water for a few hours and drained)
- 2-3 dates (pitted)
- 1 cup of water

INSTRUCTIONS:

1. Combine the lemon juice, blueberries, soaked cashews, pitted dates, and water in a blender.
2. Blend on high until the mixture is smooth and creamy.
3. Pour the Lemon-Blueberry Pie into a glass, and add a few extra blueberries on top for a pop of color.
4. Enjoy this tangy and fruity pie-inspired treat!

Chocolate Banana Dream:

INGREDIENTS:

One ripe banana

1 cup of milk of your choice (dairy or plant-based)

Two tbsp of cocoa powder

One tbsp of honey or maple syrup (adjust to taste)

1/2 tsp vanilla extract

Ice cubes

INSTRUCTIONS:

Peel the ripe banana and place it in a blender.

Add milk, cocoa powder, honey or maple syrup, and vanilla extract to the blender.

Blend quickly until all the ingredients are well combined and smooth.

Taste the Chocolate Banana Dream and adjust sweetness if needed.

Add ice cubes to the blender and pulse until the drink is chilled.

Pour the creamy and chocolaty Chocolate Banana Dream into a glass and enjoy!

Vanilla Almond Delight:

INGREDIENTS:

1 cup of almond milk or any milk of your choice

1/2 tsp pure vanilla extract

One tbsp of honey or agave syrup (adjust to taste)

Sliced almonds for garnish (optional)

INSTRUCTIONS:

Combine almond milk, vanilla extract, and honey or agave syrup in a glass.

Stir well until the sweetener is fully dissolved and the vanilla flavor is evenly distributed.

Taste and adjust sweetness if necessary.

Add a few ice cubes to the glass if you prefer a chilled drink.

Sprinkle some sliced almonds on top for added texture and nutty flavor.

Sip and savor the smooth and delightful Vanilla Almond Delight!

Strawberry Cheesecake Bliss:

INGREDIENTS:

1 cup of frOuncesen or fresh strawberries

1/2 cup of plain yogurt or Greek yogurt

1/4 cup of cream cheese

One tbsp of honey or agave syrup (adjust to taste)

1/2 tsp lemon juice

Graham cracker crumbs for garnish (optional)

INSTRUCTIONS:

Combine frOuncesen or fresh strawberries, yogurt, cream cheese, honey or agave syrup, and lemon juice in a blender.

Blend quickly until all the ingredients are well blended, and the mixture is creamy.

Taste and adjust sweetness if desired.

Pour the Strawberry Cheesecake Bliss into a glass.

Optionally, sprinkle graham cracker crumbs on top for a hint of cheesecake crust flavor.

Sip and enjoy the luscious and indulgent Strawberry Cheesecake Bliss!

Cinnamon Apple Crisp:

INGREDIENTS:

1 cup of unsweetened apple juice or cider

1/2 cup of milk of your choice (dairy or plant-based)

1/2 tsp ground cinnamon

1/4 tsp ground nutmeg

One tbsp of honey or maple syrup (adjust to taste)

Sliced apples for garnish (optional)

INSTRUCTIONS:

Heat the apple juice or cider over medium heat in a saucepan until warm.

Add milk, cinnamon, ground nutmeg, and honey or maple syrup to the saucepan.

Stir well until all the ingredients are combined and the drink is warmed.

Taste and adjust sweetness and spice levels to your liking.

Pour the Cinnamon Apple Crisp into a mug or glass.

Optionally, garnish with thinly sliced apples for a decorative touch.

Sip and enjoy the comforting and aromatic Cinnamon Apple Crisp!

Peanut Butter Cup of Magic:

INGREDIENTS:

1 cup of milk of your choice (dairy or plant-based)

Two tbsp of cocoa powder

Two tbsp of creamy peanut butter

One tbsp of honey or agave syrup (adjust to taste)

Chocolate shavings for garnish (optional)

INSTRUCTIONS:

In a saucepan, warm the milk over medium heat until it steams.

Mix cocoa powder, creamy peanut butter, and honey or agave syrup.

Whisk continuously until all the ingredients are well mixed, and the drink is smooth.

Taste and adjust sweetness if needed.

Pour the rich and decadent Peanut Butter Cup of Magic into a mug or glass.

Optionally, top with chocolate shavings for an extra chocolatey experience.

Sip and be enchanted by the delightful Peanut Butter Cup of Magic!

CLEANSING DETOX BLASTS: RENEW AND RESET

GREEN DETOX ELIXIR:

INGREDIENTS:

- 1 cup of kale (stems removed)
- One medium cucumber (peeled if not organic)
- Two stalks celery
- One green apple (cored)
- 1/2 lemon (peeled and seeded)
- Handful of fresh parsley
- 1 cup of water (optional, for desired consistency)

INSTRUCTIONS:

1. Wash all the ingredients thoroughly.
2. Chop the kale, cucumber, celery, green apple, and parsley into smaller pieces for more effortless blending.
3. Add all the ingredients to a blender.
4. Blend on high until smooth and well combined.
5. If the mixture is too thick, add water to reach your preferred consistency.
6. Pour the green detox elixir into a glass and enjoy!

BEETROOT CLEANSE:

INGREDIENTS:

- One medium-sized beetroot (peeled and chopped)
- Two medium carrots (peeled and chopped)
- 1-inch piece of fresh ginger (peeled)
- 1/2 lemon (peeled and seeded)

- 1 cup of coconut water

INSTRUCTIONS:

1. Wash and prepare all the ingredients.
2. Add the chopped beetroot, carrots, ginger, and lemon to a blender.
3. Pour in the coconut water.
4. Blend until smooth and well-mixed.
5. If the consistency is too thick, add more coconut water as desired.
6. Pour the beetroot cleanse into a glass and enjoy!

LEMON-GINGER FLUSH:

INGREDIENTS:

- One lemon (peeled and seeded)
- 1-inch piece of fresh ginger (peeled)
- Pinch of cayenne pepper (adjust to your spice preference)
- One tbsp of maple syrup
- 1 cup of water (warm, not boiling)

INSTRUCTIONS:

1. Prepare the lemon by peeling and removing the seeds.
2. Peel the ginger and cut it into smaller pieces.
3. Add the lemon, ginger, cayenne pepper, and maple syrup to a blender or a tall glass if using an immersion blender.
4. Pour in the warm water.
5. Blend or mix well until all ingredients are combined.
6. You can adjust the sweetness with more maple syrup if desired.
7. Drink the lemon-ginger flush while it's warm for best results.

DETOXIFYING DANDELION GREENS:

INGREDIENTS:

- 1 cup of dandelion greens (washed and chopped)
- One medium cucumber (peeled if not organic)
- 1 cup of fresh pineapple chunks
- Handful of fresh mint leaves
- 1 cup of coconut water

INSTRUCTIONS:

1. Wash and prepare the dandelion greens, cucumber, pineapple, and mint leaves.
2. Add all the ingredients to a blender.
3. Pour in the coconut water.
4. Blend until smooth and creamy.
5. If it's too thick, add more coconut water to reach your desired consistency.
6. Pour the dandelion green elixir into a glass and enjoy!

BERRY DETOX BLAST:

INGREDIENTS:

- 1 cup of strawberries
- 1 cup of blueberries
- One tbsp of chia seeds
- 1 cup of coconut water
- Handful of spinach leaves

INSTRUCTIONS:

1. Wash the strawberries, blueberries, and spinach leaves.

2. Add all the ingredients to a blender.
3. Blend until smooth and well combined.
4. If the consistency is too thick, add more coconut water as needed.
5. Pour the berry detox blast into a glass, and it's ready to drink!

TURMERIC CLEANSE:

INGREDIENTS:

- One tbsp of fresh turmeric (peeled and chopped) or one tsp of ground turmeric
- Two medium carrots (peeled and chopped)
- One orange (peeled and seeded)
- 1/2 lemon (peeled and seeded)
- 1 cup of filtered water

INSTRUCTIONS:

1. Wash and prepare the turmeric, carrots, orange, and lemon.
2. Add all the ingredients to a blender.
3. Pour in the filtered water.
4. Blend until smooth and well-mixed.
5. Adjust the consistency by adding more water if necessary.
6. Pour the turmeric cleanse into a glass and enjoy!

Green Goddess Cleanse:

INGREDIENTS:

1 cup of spinach leaves

One cucumber peeled and chopped

One green apple, cored and chopped

1/2 lemon, juiced

1-inch piece of ginger peeled

1 cup of water

INSTRUCTIONS:

Place all the ingredients in a blender.

Blend on high until smooth and well combined.

If the consistency is too thick, add more water until you reach your desired consistency.

Pour into a glass and enjoy!

Lemon Ginger Detoxifier: **INGREDIENTS:**

One lemon, juiced

1-inch piece of ginger, grated

One tbsp honey (optional for sweetness)

2 cups of warm water

INSTRUCTIONS:

In a mug, combine the lemon juice and grated ginger.

Add honey if desired and stir well.

Pour in the warm water and mix until the honey is dissolved.

Let it steep for a few minutes to infuse the flavors.

Sip slowly and feel refreshed!

Beetroot Clean Sweep:

INGREDIENTS:

One medium-sized beetroot, peeled and chopped

One carrot, peeled and chopped

One orange, peeled and segmented

1/2-inch piece of peeled ginger

1 cup of water

INSTRUCTIONS:

Combine all the ingredients in a blender.

Blend until smooth and well combined.

If the consistency is too thick, add more water until it's your liking.

Pour into a glass and drink up for a cleansing experience!

Pineapple Mint Reviver:

INGREDIENTS:

1 cup of fresh pineapple chunks

1/4 cup of fresh mint leaves

One tbsp of lime juice

1 cup of coconut water

INSTRUCTIONS:

Place the pineapple chunks, mint leaves, and lime juice in a blender.

Add the coconut water and blend until smooth.

Taste and adjust sweetness or tartness by adding more lime juice or a touch of honey if desired.

Pour into a glass, garnish with a mint sprig, and enjoy the tropical refreshment!

Blueberry Kale Purifier:

INGREDIENTS:

1 cup of blueberries

1 cup of chopped kale leaves (stems removed)

1/2 banana

One tbsp of chia seeds

1 cup of almond milk (or any plant-based milk)

INSTRUCTIONS:

Combine blueberries, kale, banana, chia seeds, and almond milk in a blender.

Blend until smooth and creamy.

Taste and add more sweetener (like honey or maple syrup) if desired.

Pour into a glass, top with a few extra blueberries if you like, and sip your way to a purifying experience!

NUTRIBULLET COCKTAILS: HEALTHY LIBATIONS FOR SOCIAL GATHERINGS

TROPICAL TEQUILA TANGO:

INGREDIENTS:

- 2 Ounces Tequila
- 1/2 cup of pineapple chunks
- 1/2 cup of mango chunks
- Juice of 1 lime
- 1/2 Ounces agave nectar (adjust to taste)
- Ice

INSTRUCTIONS:

1. Combine tequila, pineapple, mango, lime juice, and agave nectar in a blender.
2. Add a handful of ice to the blender.
3. Blend until smooth and well combined.
4. Taste and adjust sweetness with more agave nectar if desired.
5. Pour the Tropical Tequila Tango into a glass, garnish with a slice of lime or pineapple, and enjoy!

MOJITO TWIST:

INGREDIENTS:

- 2 Ounces White rum

- 6-8 fresh mint leaves
- Juice of 1 lime
- 4-5 slices of cucumber
- Sparkling water (club soda)
- Ice
- Sugar or simple syrup (optional for added sweetness)

INSTRUCTIONS:

1. Muddle the mint leaves and cucumber slices in a cocktail shaker to release their flavors.
2. Add the white rum and lime juice to the shaker.
3. If you prefer a sweeter drink, add a dash of sugar or simple syrup at this stage.
4. Fill the shaker with ice and shake well.
5. Strain the mixture into a glass filled with ice.
6. Top off the glass with sparkling water (club soda).
7. Garnish with a sprig of fresh mint and a slice of lime.
8. Stir gently and enjoy your refreshing Mojito Twist!

BERRY VODKA CRUSH:

INGREDIENTS:

- 2 Ounces Vodka
- 1/2 cup of mixed berries (strawberries, blueberries, raspberries, etc.)
- Juice of 1 lime
- Club soda
- Ice

INSTRUCTIONS:

1. In a cocktail shaker, muddle the mixed berries to release their juices.

2. Add the vodka and lime juice to the shaker.
3. Fill the shaker with ice and shake well.
4. Strain the mixture into a glass filled with ice.
5. Top off the glass with club soda.
6. Please give it a gentle stir to mix the flavors.
7. Garnish with a lime slice or some fresh berries.
8. Sip and enjoy your Berry Vodka Crush!

SPICY PALOMA PUNCH:

INGREDIENTS:

- 2 Ounces Tequila
- 1/2 cup of grapefruit juice
- 2-3 slices of fresh jalapeño (seeds removed for less heat)
- Juice of 1 lime
- 1/2 Ounces agave nectar (adjust to taste)
- Ice
- Club soda

INSTRUCTIONS:

1. In a cocktail shaker, muddle the jalapeño slices to release their spiciness.
2. Add tequila, grapefruit, lime, and agave nectar to the shaker.
3. Fill the shaker with ice and shake well.
4. Strain the mixture into a glass filled with ice.
5. Top off the glass with club soda.
6. Stir gently to combine the flavors.
7. Garnish with a slice of grapefruit or a jalapeño wheel (optional).
8. Sip and savor the Spicy Paloma Punch!

CUCUMBER GIN REFRESHER:

INGREDIENTS:

- 2 Ounces Gin
- 4-5 slices of cucumber
- 6-8 fresh mint leaves
- Juice of 1 lime
- Tonic water
- Ice

INSTRUCTIONS:

1. In a cocktail shaker, muddle the cucumber slices and mint leaves.
2. Add the gin and lime juice to the shaker.
3. Fill the shaker with ice and shake well.
4. Strain the mixture into a glass filled with ice.
5. Top off the glass with tonic water.
6. Stir gently to mix the flavors.
7. Garnish with a cucumber slice and a sprig of mint.
8. Sip and enjoy the calm and refreshing Cucumber Gin Refresher!

POMEGRANATE WHISKEY SOUR:

INGREDIENTS:

- 2 Ounces Whiskey
- 1/2 cup of pomegranate juice
- Juice of 1 lemon
- 1/2 Ounces simple syrup (adjust to taste)
- Ice

INSTRUCTIONS:

1. Combine the whiskey, pomegranate juice, lemon juice, and simple syrup in a cocktail shaker.
2. Fill the shaker with ice and shake well.
3. Strain the mixture into a glass filled with ice.
4. Garnish with a lemon slice or a few pomegranate arils.
5. Sip and enjoy the delightful Pomegranate Whiskey Sour!

TROPICAL TURMERIC TWIST:

INGREDIENTS:

- 1 cup of fresh pineapple chunks
- One ripe mango, peeled and diced
- One tsp of ground turmeric (or 1-inch piece of fresh turmeric, peeled)
- 1/2 tsp ground cinnamon
- 1 cup of coconut water
- Ice cubes (optional)

INSTRUCTIONS:

1. Combine pineapple, mango, turmeric, cinnamon, and coconut water in a blender.
2. Blend until smooth and creamy.
3. Add some ice cubes and blend again if you prefer a chilled drink.
4. Pour into a glass, garnish with a slice of pineapple or a sprinkle of ground cinnamon, and enjoy the tropical twist!

BERRY MOJITO MADNESS:

INGREDIENTS:

- 1 cup of mixed berries (strawberries, blueberries, raspberries, blackberries)
- 1/4 cup of fresh mint leaves
- One lime, juiced
- One tbsp honey or agave nectar (adjust to taste)
- 1 cup of sparkling water or Club soda
- Ice cubes

INSTRUCTIONS:

1. In a tall glass, muddle the mixed berries and fresh mint leaves together with a spoon or a muddler.
2. Add lime juice and honey (or agave nectar) and stir until well combined.
3. Fill the glass with ice cubes.
4. Pour the sparkling water or club soda over the top.
5. Please gently stir and garnish with a mint sprig and some additional berries.
6. Sip and feel refreshed with this berry-infused mojito mocktail!

CUCUMBER GINGER REFRESHER:

INGREDIENTS:

- One medium cucumber peeled and sliced
- 1-inch piece of ginger peeled
- One lime, juiced
- One tbsp of honey or maple syrup (adjust to taste)
- 2 cups of water
- Ice cubes

INSTRUCTIONS:

1. Combine the cucumber slices, ginger, lime juice, honey (or maple syrup), and water in a blender.
2. Blend until smooth.
3. Strain the mixture through a fine mesh strainer into a pitcher to remove solids.
4. Add ice cubes to the pitcher and stir.
5. Pour into glasses, garnish with a cucumber slice or lime wheel, and enjoy the calm and refreshing refreshment!

SPICY WATERMELON PUNCH:

INGREDIENTS:

- 2 cups of fresh watermelon cubes (seeds removed)
- 1/2 jalapeno pepper (seeds removed for less heat)
- One lime, juiced
- One tbsp honey or agave nectar (adjust to taste)
- 1 cup of cold water
- Ice cubes

INSTRUCTIONS:

1. Combine watermelon cubes, jalapeno pepper, lime juice, honey (or agave nectar), and water in a blender.
2. Blend until smooth.
3. Taste and adjust sweetness or spiciness as needed.
4. Strain the mixture through a fine mesh strainer into a pitcher to remove any pulp or seeds.
5. Add ice cubes to the pitcher and stir well.
6. Pour into glasses, garnish with a small slice of watermelon or a lime wedge, and enjoy the zesty watermelon punch!

POMEGRANATE BASIL FIZZ:

INGREDIENTS:

- 1 cup of pomegranate juice
- 1/4 cup of fresh basil leaves
- One tbsp of lime juice
- One tbsp honey or agave nectar (adjust to taste)
- Sparkling water or club soda
- Pomegranate arils and fresh basil leaves for garnish
- Ice cubes

INSTRUCTIONS:

1. Combine pomegranate juice, fresh basil leaves, lime juice, and honey (or agave nectar) in a blender.
2. Blend until the basil leaves are well incorporated.
3. Strain the mixture through a fine mesh strainer into a tall glass filled with ice cubes.
4. Top off the glass with sparkling water or club soda.
5. Stir gently and garnish with pomegranate arils and a few fresh basil leaves.
6. Sip and enjoy the effervescent pomegranate basil fizz!

Printed in Great Britain
by Amazon